THE LIE THAT IS LINCOLN

THE LIE THAT IS LINCOLN

*To Pat
with warmest
regards*

[signature]
Stephen Miklosik, M.D.

Copyright © 2012 by Stephen Miklosik, M.D..

Library of Congress Control Number: 2012901244
ISBN: Hardcover 978-1-4691-5641-5
Softcover 978-1-4691-5640-8
Ebook 978-1-4691-5642-2

All rights reserved. No part of this book may be reproduced or transmitted in any form or by any means, electronic or mechanical, including photocopying, recording, or by any information storage and retrieval system, without permission in writing from the copyright owner.

This book was printed in the United States of America.

To order additional copies of this book, contact:
Xlibris Corporation
1-888-795-4274
www.Xlibris.com
Orders@Xlibris.com

DEDICATION

This book is dedicated to the memory of my parents, John and Suzi (Kusnier) Miklosik, whose legacy handed down to their children was the concept of social Darwinism, i.e., of survival of the fittest in the face of all adversities. Born in the Austro-Hungarian Empire (now Slovakia) at the beginning of the twentieth century, acquiring a meager education in Hungarian-speaking schools, realizing that opportunity in immigrating to North America, they borrowed money from friends and in a helter-skelter trip landed in Halifax, Nova Scotia. From there they were transported to Western Canada during the teeth of the Depression working as farm laborers.

Hearing through the grapevine from other Slovaks of better prospects in Port Colborne, Ontario, my father eventually got a job at a nickel plant (International Nickel Co. or Inco). Obsessing that education was the key to success in life, their sons John (engineer), Stephen (MD), and Andrew (engineer) were the crown jewels of their existence.

As a retired anesthesiologist in Columbus, Ohio, and now having much time to read, I was struck and shocked by the events of the American Civil War: how so many Americans (North and South) died needlessly for an insignificant purpose, how the historians continue to insist it was for a noble purpose, and that Abraham Lincoln was one of our greatest presidents. Bullshit! And this book tells why!

Before I forget, let me also dedicate this book to my dear wife, Mary Anne, whose patience over all these years of living with a curmudgeon (me) can only be described as exemplary, if not saintly.

INTRO
ICONOCLASTIC

That this book will undoubtedly be described as iconoclastic is a given that I accept with pride and satisfaction. Once the deception that Lincoln was a secular saint is revealed and uncovered, then the truth will show the unvarnished nature of the man. His reputation is built upon the idealism and compassion toward the Negro race when he emancipated them from the oppression of his slave controllers: masters, overseers, buyers, and sellers. It is buttressed by the clever propaganda by the Lincoln admirers and ass-kissers who perpetrated and perpetuated the bullshit that he "saved the nation" and that he was the "redeemer president." To this very day, his sycophants and acolytes work assiduously not only to maintain but also to enhance his saintly image. These criminals continue the *great lie*!

That he was a clever wordsmith who enhanced his legal and political stature through his oratorical and debating skills is undeniable. That, in his soul, he lacked those skills of compromise. Of give and take and adaptation are undeniable, as his monomaniacal pursuit of death and destruction reveal. That his vengeful lust plunged the nation into an unnecessary bloodbath, sacrificing between 600,000 and one million brave souls (depending upon which statistics you read) in order to free four million slaves, also undeniable.

Perhaps it is a stretch when I compare myself with George Orwell's writings, but insofar as to his "reverence for the truth" goes, I claim to be his equal. What I have written here is directly contrary to the received writings of the established class of historians, but I claim theirs is, put simply, bullshit that was cleverly promulgated to hide the stark reality of that monstrous crime—the American Civil War! I further include myself in Christopher Hitchens's assessment of Orwell when he opines, "But he's not in the first rank of writers. And that's a good thing, because it shows what average, ordinary people can do if they care to, and it abolishes some of the alibis and excuses for people who aren't brave." Thus, buttressed by these two viewpoints, my assertion seems less ridiculous.

CRITICAL THINKING

Many historians have gone to great lengths to study and analyze why some people have the capacity for critical thinking while others have not. They have debated the age-old question of heredity versus environment, and I have tended to conclude that dispassionate people, i.e., those who are distrustful of intuition and emotion and relying on reason and empiricism, are more likely to have better critical faculties. These are people who are curious, open-minded, of doubting-Thomas orientation, open to new experiences but careful to keep their emotions under control. By relying on reason and empiricism, they arrive at conclusions more closely parallel to reality.

I, in addition, feel my critical thinking originates in my innate ability to recognize bullshit when I see it or hear it. Is this heredity or acquired? I don't know and I don't care! In the case of the American Civil War, I find it incongruous that despite the carnage—the loss of over 1,000,000 American cream of its youth, wasted for apparently no good reason—the man who instigated and perpetuated this bloodbath is considered a secular saint and a moral compass to the world. Bullshit! He was a backwoods, barroom brawler, a clone of the Hatfield/McCoy clans, whose belligerent nature, infuriated by the punch-in-the-nose at Bull Run (Manassas) impelled him on his four-year downslide until Appomattox. A Greek tragedy writ large!

As a naturalized American, Canadian born of Slovak descent, I am somewhat familiar with the creation, birth, and/or "union" of Czechoslovakia and with the creation of other nation states of Eastern Europe in the aftermath of World War I. It should be emphasized that the role of Woodrow Wilson was instrumental in this regard. In studying for my citizenship exam, I became aware of certain parallelisms with that of my parents' native country. In the creation and/or "union" of both nations, two similar, yet dissimilar, cultures were blended into one nation. Just as the industrial Czechs were united with the agrarian Slovaks, so too the industrial North was united with the agrarian South. Yet it may be said that both halves of each nation possessed features, primarily language, that contributed to a reasonably stable marriage, lasting eighty-five years for the United States, and seventy-four for Czechoslovakia.

The contrast, however, lies in the method of their respective attempts at separation. Despite the friction, animosity, and resentment between the two, the Czechs and Slovaks managed a peaceful resolution to their conflict: a no-fault divorce if you will, a "velvet revolution." In stark contrast, the Americans could and would not agree to a divorce under any circumstances! Where Vaclav Havel, possessing a distaste for confrontation, was magnanimous and charitable in his dealings with the Slovaks, allowed the nation to separate; whereas Abraham Lincoln, a man who relished confrontation, led the nation down the bloody path to war and preserved the "union." I do not believe there were any casualties in the Czechoslovak rupture. America, on the other hand, suffered between 600,000 and one million casualties. Yet the historians persist in portraying Abraham Lincoln as this nation's secular saint. What pure unadulterated bullshit!

Having entered the United States at age thirty and not having been subjected to brainwashing from an early age on the sainthood of Abraham Lincoln, I claim to have a dispassionate, sanguine, Spock-like view of American history. The following is an iconoclastic analysis and presentation on the stupidity of the American Civil War in which Abraham Lincoln, an uncompromising zealot with a callous indifference to the loss of 1,000,000 lives, pursued a murderous course with dictatorial powers.

The great industrialist Henry Ford, not noted as a philosopher, might have made the most accurate and acerbic observation when he said, "History is bunk." In the twenty-first century, he might have been cruder and said, "History is crap" or "History is bullshit." Orwell's negative view was "History is written by the ruling classes." Historians insist the accuracy of history for it is mostly written right after the fact when it was fresh in everyone's minds. My contention to this is that in wars, history is written by the victorious side whereas "losers'" accounts rarely see the light of day!

The acolytes of the Lincoln flame, beginning with his cabinet, jealously nurtured and guarded the foundation upon which Lincoln's reputation is built. Once Edwin Stanton uttered, "He now belongs to the ages," the Lincoln-adulation-industry was born. Like sheep following the Judas goat, the subsequent historians fell into line genuflecting at the altar of Lincolnmania and perpetuating the myth of secular sainthood; this despite the fact that he was an attorney/politician who spent the major part of his life either running for or serving in political office. He knew where power lay!

That I view the world according to my own criteria and not as others would have me view it, marching to my own drummer's beat, being an independent thinker, a ruthless iconoclastic reasoner, sets me aside from the herd. When most people visit historic battle sites, as the Vicksburg National Cemetery, holding the largest number of Civil War dead—17,000—they are moved emotionally by the thoughts of the heroic struggle that occurred. I, on the other hand, think of the horrendous loss of life for little purpose, of the sounds and smell of gunpowder, the cries of the dying, the overwhelming stench of the dead and dying. Why? Why? Why? How did seemingly sane people allow themselves to become so enraged as to become brothers killing brothers? What leaders, madmen drunk with boundless power, would force their citizens into this hellish meat grinder of death and destruction? Who but a butcher would sacrifice so many lives for such a minor cause as slavery? Others solved the issue of slavery in a sane bloodless way. Why couldn't we?

DISCLAIMER

Before we go too far in this presentation let me first reveal to the world that I am not a historian, merely a student of that subject but with a suspicious, skeptical, and contrarian outlook on what I read, both within and between the lines. Thus, I do not subscribe to the necessary discipline that historians are subject to and I'm, therefore, free to pursue my own jaundiced and cynical view of history and not one laid down by members of a discriminating and incestuous club jealously guarding their prerogatives as exclusive territory.

Second, as an immigrant to this great country (from Canada at age thirty), I feel possessed of a dispassionate, untainted perspective entirely different from those born here. They are known to have been exposed and subjected to an early and frequent bombardment of history favorable in outlook to Saint Abraham Lincoln. What was most disturbing to me was the cavalier attitude of historians to the loss of over 1,000,000 Americans (North and South) in the American Civil War, serenely portrayed as a heroic enterprise with so many young men proudly marching forth to kill and die. Nowhere do we get a sense of the harsh reality of events, the horrific nature of the battles, the violent convulsions, the exsanguinating ferocity and butchery, and the stupidity of the whole enterprise.

Through the influence of my long years as an amateur historian I am inclined to agree with a few observations by some noted historians and writers. "History is never a closed book or a final verdict. It is always in the making," wrote Arthur Schlesinger Jr. "The one duty we owe to history," said Oscar Wilde, "is to rewrite it." Perhaps he should have added "for removing or correcting errors." With specific regards to the American Civil War, I agree with James G. Randall and Charles Beard that it was caused by a "blundering generation" driven by fanaticism, especially by the fanaticism of the abolitionists who transformed a "repressive conflict" into a "needless war."

I am inclined to agree with some historians but only with reference to the American Civil War that there is no difference between history and fiction. The fiction (or bullshit) that the original historians foisted upon the American public with subsequent sycophantic historians who perpetuated that fraud to this very day.

And I strongly disagree with those historians who have the arrogance that they are the sole purveyors of that subject and that history is what they say it is!

IN FLANDERS FIELDS

In Flanders fields the poppies blow
Between the crosses, row on row,
That mark our place; and in the sky
The larks, still bravely singing, fly
Scarce heard among the guns below.

We are the dead. Short days ago
We lived, felt dawn, saw sunset glow,
Loved, and were loved, and now we lie
In Flanders fields.

Take up our quarrel with the foe:
To you from failing hands we throw
The torch; be yours to hold it high.
If ye break faith with us who die
We shall not sleep, though poppies grow
In Flanders fields.

    This beautiful and poignant poem, expressing the overwhelming sadness in the deaths of so many allied combatants in the First World War, was written by Lt. Col. John McCrae, a graduate of my medical school at the University of Toronto; he in 1898, I in 1960. Perhaps he and I have a kinship through our compassionate view of life; that we could see the utter tragedy of war, that so many young lives were snuffed out in their prime for no apparent good reason. We both treasured life too much for, in all its vagaries and vicissitudes, it is pure folly to waste it in the pursuit of some obscure idealism. This is my emphatic view in totality with regards to the American Civil War.

WHERE SELDOM IS HEARD A NEGATIVE WORD

In all my years of reading about Abraham Lincoln, no one, and I mean no one, has had the nerve to utter a negative or derogatory word against this man. Without exception, all the accounts on Lincoln's life, from beginning to end, have been nothing but laudatory. Therefore a quote by Christopher Hitchens, in the March 2006 issue of *The Atlantic*, came as an unexpected surprise for me for it articulated my sentiments precisely. Perry Anderson is said to have made an utterance which many historians would consider as blasphemous. Hitchens says (on page 133): "A few years ago, when we jointly addressed a gathering in New York, he startled me by announcing that he thought that the confederacy should have been allowed to secede. His reasoning was elegant enough—slavery was historically doomed in any case; two semi-continental states would have been more natural; American expansionism would have been checked; Lincoln was a bloodthirsty Bismarckian etatiste and megalomaniac, but it was nonetheless remarkable to hear such a direct attack on the thinking and writing of Marx and Engels, who had been 100 per cent for Lincoln and the Union and who had identified America as the country of future progress as surely as they had located Russia as the heartland of backwardness and despotism."

Thus in reading this book, the gentle reader might become disturbed by my aggressive, dismissive approach, by the iconoclastic attack upon the long-held cherished image of the saintly Abraham Lincoln, a fabrication that has been rammed down our throats beginning by Edwin M. Stanton's "now he belongs to the ages" and perpetuated by historians ever since. It is a fact there were over one million casualties in the American Civil War! The largest family feud ever! Abraham Lincoln was a stubborn, uncompromising, tyrannical butcher, and to anyone who tries to defend this sad record I say "bullshit" and get outta here. I have the facts and you have the bullshit. Somebody named Boake Carter said truth is "the first casualty of war" and so it was in regards to Abraham Lincoln! Over the many years, we have been fed a lot of bullshit on Abraham Lincoln and I refuse to swallow any of it!

THE AMERICAN CIVIL WAR

Tragedy—"A serious drama having a sorrowful or disastrous conclusion."

Calamity—"A state of deep distress or misery caused by major misfortune or loss"

—"An extraordinary grave event marked by great loss and lasting distress and affliction."

Disaster—"A sudden great misfortune, especially the one bringing with it destruction of life or property causing complete ruin."

Cataclysm—"A violent social or political upheaval."

Any and/or all of the above definitions are valid descriptions of the American Civil War!

Noted historian Bruce Catton said it all when he observed, "Few Civil War battles cost more or meant less."

From some saner thinkers of the enlightenment, polite conversation represented one of the few societal conventions keeping civilization from degenerating into disunion and civil war!

Whenever I sit down at home in my easy chair during my quiet hours and contemplate all of the circumstances surrounding the American Civil War, I always become severely depressed for I have concluded it to have been an unmitigated human tragedy, a disaster of gargantuan proportions. To me it was a Hatfield-McCoy family feud writ large, a blood dispute of brothers, fathers, and sons killing each other for no good reason. Never in world history, other than in America, can we find any examples where slavery was of sufficient significance, importance, or impact that it required the slaughter and sacrifice of over 1,000,000 young souls to bring about its demise. In my humble opinion, the "problem" of man's total exploitation of man (slavery) is never bad enough to require such severe measures as the horrendous bloodletting of the Civil War. Who really is the villain? Is it the slave owner, the slave driver, and the slave trader, or is it the butcher of the slave owner, the slave driver, and the slave trader? It is most certainly the latter, and you cannot convince me otherwise! It is to the backwoods primitives that compromise, dialogue, and discourse seem to be alien attributes in dealing with problems but immediate, senseless, and unending butchery is not! Even the great abolitionist Frederick Douglas questioned whether a postwar devotion to black freedom would redeem the war or whether the loss of over 1,000,000 souls would "pass into history a miserable failure, barren of permanent results—a scandalous and shocking waste of blood and treasure."

THE LIFE AND TIMES OF ABRAHAM LINCOLN—A GREEK TRAGEDY

The dictionary defines a tragedy as a serious drama having a sorrowful or disastrous outcome. From other sources, we learn that it originated with the ancient Greeks, and it is characterized by a circumscribed and fixed formula. Examples of modern-day dramas have many features that are reminiscent of the original Greek formulation.

The characters of Greek tragedies are heroic ones—royalty, famous historical figures, or other notable people—but all with exceptional attributes and abilities. Never common people. They are impelled by these qualities and talents, moved to actions that end disastrously in some form of calamity, often by death.

The themes are about moral, philosophical, or religious significance. The tragedy deals with serious human actions, issues with insights into human nature. They often explore questions of morality, the meaning of human existence, the relationships between people or between people and their gods. These heroic characters seem to be victims of violent passions, usually their own, which they cannot control. The performance is characterized also by powerful, almost poetic dialogue.

In the end the main character has died or lost his or her loved ones. In Aristotle's definition of a Greek tragedy, he talks of a "catharsis" in viewing this performance. An emotional or psychological release, a purification, rousing emotions of pity or fear.

Therefore in taking into account the vast scope of Abraham Lincoln's life, it seems logical that, in the hands of any competent dramatist, an excellent drama along the lines of a Greek tragedy could be written for the theater-going public. All the elements are there! Although he was of humble log-cabin origin, by hard work and application, he achieved heroic stature. By his up-by-the-boot-straps self-education, he raised himself to be a successful attorney/politician and finally as president of the United States of America.

He was forced to deal with a national crisis, wrestling with moral considerations of the concomitant existence of slavery in a democracy. National Union was preserved by the troops in many bloody, horrific battles. As the denouement arrived, military victory, the hero of this historical episode loses his life by tragic assassination. Great was the mourning! Great was the Aristotelian "catharsis"!

Some cynic, probably one with enormous dictatorial power, has made the profound observation that, in order to make an omelet, it is necessary to break a few eggs! Consistent with, and following along, this train of thought, when one might naturally conclude that Abraham Lincoln not only smashed all the eggs within his reach but also destroyed all the nests, killed all the chickens, and, finally, for good measure, burned down the chicken coop! Surely one must ask, with disgusted impertinence, why? Why did he have to pursue such a path of unadulterated carnage, sacrificing the lives of over 1,000,000 Americans in the process?

Many historians follow the party line and tell us that he had to take such an outrageous course in order to "save the Union." Many historians apparently have swallowed this bullshit, hook, line, and sinker, and persist in spreading it to all who would listen. To them, preserving the Union at all costs was a noble and heroic gesture. Had he not pursued this goal with such vehemence, savagery, and butchery, according to Lincoln and his supporters, the whole noble novel experiment in "democracy" would have been doomed to total and abject failure. That he "'saved' the Union" is nothing but pure propaganda, a subterfuge that hides the hideousness of the carnage that is called the American Civil War!

I am speaking on behalf of the 1,000,000 wasted American souls dumped unceremoniously in American soil, out of sight, out of mind, their potentialities rotting with their carcasses under the cold ground. Their voices cry out in muffled frustration and anger that they gave up their lives needlessly for a dubious and/or insignificant cause. Wasted, wasted, wasted! Young lives full of vigor and promise like butchered budding flowers never to bloom in ordained beauteous fullness. The stench of thousands of bodies decomposing in full view, overwhelming those whose painful task was to quickly hide them from human gaze and before the crows and vultures could violate their sanctity!

That America lost so many brave souls, especially much of the cream of its manhood, seems not to concern the majority of historians. That it was an unnecessary loss makes it all the more tragic and poignant. Damn those historians for their imbecility!

To me the five-volume set by Carl Sandburg is considered the definitive biography on Abraham Lincoln. It is the "revealed wisdom" or the virtual biblical revelation of his exemplary life handed down for future generations to echo and laud the mythological accounts of his exploitations, both as a backwoods lawyer and as a president. Except for the vehement attacks by the Southern press during the Civil War, no dispassionate critical analysis of this secular saint can be found.

The contrived portraiture of a brooding, melancholy figure with all the weight of the world's problems on his shoulders have been carefully crafted and preserved to garner the world's sympathies. He is the benevolent, caring, compassionate father-figure impelled by the certainty that slavery was the distilled essence of evil and that the "holy grail," i.e., the Union, *must* be pursued and preserved. Yet we are told he was possessed of an inflexible will, stronger than the finest steel, together with an equally strong stubbornness that allowed him to persevere four long bloody and agonizing years in pursuit of his monomaniacal goal: Union!

No one seems to have paid attention to the fact that he possessed two major character flaws that should have disqualified him from consideration for secular sainthood: he was an attorney and a politician! And through insane pursuit of "union at all costs," he wasted the lives of 1,000,000 innocents.

Virtually all the events of the American Civil War continue to be a treasure trove, a cornucopia, a gold mine for both the professional and amateur historians. Books, magazines, articles, and television documentaries make a lot of money for these people as they continually and repeatedly bombard us with this painful aspect of our past. With their writings they force us to revisit each and every battle, relive the agonies of battles lost and won, of comrades fallen; husbands, fathers, brothers, and betrotheds lost in a futile attempt at victory and subjugation, visiting the thousands of graves in hundreds of historic cemeteries made sacred by the hundreds of thousands of gallons of blood spilled and wasted on the battleground. Yet the butcheries went on and on and on without a pause or slowdown.

And we ask ourselves: "What was this bloodletting all about?" If we ignore the bullshit about the noble aim of "preserving the Union," we are left with the unvarnished truth. It was the deliberate manipulation of white peoples' emotions by arousing their compassion toward the oppressed slaves by arousing their guilt over man exploiting man for pecuniary reasons and by arousing their pity and sorrow at the unfortunate condition of the Negro slave. Once the American mind had been sufficiently programmed by the maudlin presentation but by the fantastic success of the world's greatest piece of propaganda, Harriet Beecher Stowe's *Uncle Tom's Cabin* then Abraham Lincoln's task of moving the nation to war was made very easy. With a messianic impulse and righteous indignation Lincoln, Grant, Sherman, and Sheridan, the new four horsemen of the apocalypse swept through the South like alien hordes, leaving death and destruction in their wakes.

INTRO REALITY

Taking a page out of popular TV's obsession with reality shows, the history channels too should introduce and expose the nation to the brutal realities of the American Civil War! Too long has this nation been seduced by the deliberate fiction that this war was a noble enterprise undertaken by high-minded Christians of the North and fought for a general principle. They were led by a secular saint Abraham Lincoln, intent upon relieving Negro slaves from that harsh and "sinful" oppression: slavery. Too long have the harsh realities of a Hatfield-McCoy family feud, writ large, been portrayed as a minor disruption in the evolution of the American democratic spirit. The unprecedented carnage should be revealed and emphasized that over 1,000,000 American souls had their lives wasted because the brute Lincoln, and his equally brutal cabinet, resolutely pushed this nation into this slaughter machine. Yet this astonishing massacre, and virtual genocide, has been cleverly hidden by the politicians and overlooked and ignored by the established class of historians.

The true character of the American Civil War should be revealed to the whole world in its harshest reality of a stomach-churning evocation of military slaughter. Here in the twenty-first century, the American people are chagrined to hear of the loss of 3,000 American souls in Iraq and Afghanistan yet we are led to believe that the loss of over 1,000,000 in the Civil War evoked no such consternation in the nation during and afterward.

I am inclined to follow the philosophical outlook of Samuel Butler who once wrote, "I never write on any subject unless I believe the opinion of those who have the ear of the public to be mistaken, and this involves, as a necessary consequence that every book I write runs counter to the men who are in possession of the field; hence I am always in hot water."

MACHIAVELLIAN BEHAVIOR OF ABRAHAM LINCOLN

By his behavior prior to and during the Civil War, I am under the firm conviction that Abraham Lincoln was either unfamiliar with, or totally ignored, the pronunciations found in the Declaration of Independence and the Constitution. Except for "all men are created equal," he tended not to recognize state's rights nor any philosophical understanding of self-determination of free peoples.

His behavior, instead, tended to show a remarkable familiarity with the writings of Niccolo Machiavelli especially those found in *The Ruler* particularly the chapter "The Pledges of Rulers." Several of Machiavelli's statements, moreover, seemed to have been written with Abraham Lincoln in mind. For instance, in dealing with the situation as Lincoln found himself, Machiavelli observes, "Now there are two ways of resolving conflict, violence and the law; the latter is the proper method over men, the former for beasts," but he goes on "since the law is often inadequate for the purpose, it becomes necessary to have a recourse to violence. A ruler must nicely judge the proportion of man to beast required." Later, "we can conclude that a ruler need not be endowed with all the good qualities... but he should *seem* to possess them."

"Circumstances may compel a ruler, particularly one recently established, for the preservation of his state to act against the principles which men call good... to break his word, to be ruthless, tyrannical and an enemy of religion." Further, he should stick to righteousness when he can, but be prepared to do evil when he must." He concludes it paramount "that he appear the paragon of mercy, good faith, honesty, kindness and godliness. Generally speaking, men judge more by appearances than by realities."

"The mass of humanity is taken in by appearances, the minority has access to the reality, and the minority will not dare to be in conflict with public opinion backed by all the authority of the state. Where there is no court to judge men's actions, particularly the actions of despots, their results provide the verdict. If a ruler succeeds in defense and preservation of the state, his acts will always be held honorable and praiseworthy. The vulgar mind is always ready to accept appearances and results, and the crowd is nothing if not vulgar, and the discriminating few are elbowed out by crowds."

It can, thus, be concluded by the above references how these descriptions apply to the brutal methods used by Abraham Lincoln in crushing the revolt of the South, yet appearing to all the world as a secular saint. All the historians have been seduced by the appearances of goodness in the man, praised him and continue to do so to this very day ad nauseum.

DISPASSIONATE ANALYSIS

The study of American history reveals that nothing stirred the passions of its citizenry as did the issue of slavery. Verbal assaults led to impassioned defenses that led to more vehement attacks progressively escalating the back-and-forth anger till it erupted in the greatest of fratricides we call the Civil War. As an outsider, an immigrant from Canada, of Slovak ancestry, I maintain to be an impartial, dispassionate observer and analyst of this cataclysmic event. Because of this and because I was not bombarded by the incessant propaganda and brainwashing of Lincolnmania that American children are exposed to, therefore, my analysis is not tainted. "History is bunk" observed Henry Ford, being too polite to use the vernacular "bullshit."

Much as the character Spock (of Starship Enterprise) I would hope our analysis would dissect and present a conclusion devoid of preconceived ideologies, and because of this contrarian view, some might accuse me of being politically incorrect when I do not follow the party line. First of all, let me begin with the heretical viewpoint that is contrary to the received wisdom that slavery was an abomination, a sin against Christian teachings and, most importantly, in the eyes of God. Historians and archeologists reveal to us this exploitation of man by man, where one man owned another and had complete control and domination over him has been known to have existed since the dawn of civilization or at least 10,000 years ago. This entity, called slavery, reached its peak in ancient Egyptian, Greek, and Roman civilizations, declining during the middle ages, then had a resurgence in the 1500s and 1600s with the European discovery of the New World. Here, because of the availability of fertile gargantuan estates, a labor force that could function in the hot and humid climate became paramount and this, happily, could easily be found and exploited from the African continent. As the demand for this labor exceeded the supply, the slave industry exploded to accommodate the needs of the plantar class of the South.

Thus, in the long history of this habit, the concept of evil, immorality, and sin that has become associated with it, is of relatively recent origin in the 1800s in America. Led by the "compassionates" or abolitionists with their escalated rhetoric, the activity took on the appearance of a moral crusade on behalf of the downtrodden, exploited slaves. In my humble opinion, the portrayal of grossly inhumane treatment of the slaves in Harriet Beecher Stowe's *Uncle Tom's Cabin* is a vile canard, but the greatest propaganda coup the world has ever known, putting to shame the amateur attempts of Adolf Hitler's propaganda minister Joseph Goebbels. The enormous psychological impact her book had upon the nation, and even the world, cannot be underestimated; it continues to resonate in the consciences of Americans to this very day. Throughout the world, her vivid descriptions made the readers "familiar" with life on the plantation and were moved to tears by the deaths of Little Eva and Uncle Tom; also the name Simon Legree has become identified with evil incarnate.

Stowe's opus moved the nation to tears, to be resolute against this evil slavery, by her maudlin bathos masquerading as events which actually occurred on a daily basis on all slave plantations. Through her pen she propelled the nation as an avalanche hurtling down a mountainside to crash into a bloody heap that was known as the most uncivil of civil wars! This is not my attribution, it is Abraham Lincoln's, for upon meeting her for the first time in the White House he is to have said, "So this is the lady who wrote the book that made this great war." Ironically, even if unintentionally, Lincoln admits that slavery was indeed *the* cause of the Civil War! Though the historians tend to obfuscate this fact by asserting, "No! It was to preserve the Union!" Because this revelation came directly from the horse's mouth, it should silence all of them forever!

In summary, looking at the big picture in this Civil War, Abraham Lincoln and his major accomplice, Harriet Beecher Stowe, should be charged with crimes against humanity. As major instigators of the Civil War, they were responsible for the deaths of over 1,000,000 young Americans who were sent on a wild goose chase in search of a bloody solution to the problem of slavery simply because the leadership in the nation was deficient in knowledge and skills to arrive at a solution using diplomacy with give-and-take compromise. Or, once recognizing a total impasse to a satisfactory resolution, the North should have recognized the South's right to their own liberty and personal freedom, a natural right for each and every human being!

SLAVISH HISTORY

Because their deaths are viewed as untimely, that their goals were not totally fulfilled, assassinated leaders throughout history became larger than life to historians as they assess the accomplishments of these men. From Julius Caesar through Abraham Lincoln and JFK, we are left saddened as we contemplate what might have been—the promise of unfulfilled plans and dreams and unrealized potential. Abraham Lincoln's mythological status is unparalleled and indelibly fixed in our minds, even now, by the slavish obsession of historians. Their incessant adulation cultivated and created an aura about the man of such heroic and noble stature sufficient to consider him for elevation to secular sainthood. Even to this very day, they fall in line as automatons, one behind the other, in rapt adoration, pledging themselves to worship forever at the altar of Saint Abraham, the savior of the nation!

Not one historian can be found critical of the man! None of these historians can find any flaws in the man! No one sees, as a result of his misguided, unwavering policies to crush the South, the resultant death and destruction and enormous waste of North and South American lives. None describes in detail the stench of thousands upon thousands of corpses rotting in the battlefields. Where are the independent, dispassionate, and unbiased historians ready to describe the Civil War as an unmitigated disaster? It was not a heroic struggle but barbaric carnage brought on by a rigid, vengeful tyrant drunk with power and unwilling to compromise. It was the modern-day example of a pyrrhic victory to be remembered forever with sadness and remorse!

IMPETUS

IMPETUS

In studying for American citizenship exam and having read much about the American Civil War, plus having visited Gettysburg, I became appalled at the tragic waste of so many human lives to achieve the "preservation of the Union." History books were inconsistent in their reporting of the casualties but generally concluded the number to be about 600,000. To my amazement and consternation, the January 30–Febraury 6, 2006, issue of the *U.S. News* revealed to me that the losses for the Union were 646,392 and for the Confederacy 335,524. It is mind-boggling to me that over one million brave young men were sacrificed merely to liberate around four million slaves! In addition the cost of the war was reported as $5.2 billion, equivalent to $62 billion in 2002 currency, another mind-boggling figure!

Born with a suspicious and skeptical attitude, developed over the years and endowed with an iconoclastic nature, I have concluded, after prolonged, careful and deliberate consideration that Abraham Lincoln was, in fact, a monomaniacal butcher who plunged the nation into an unnecessary bloodbath because he did not have the patience for the long and laborious process of negotiation necessary to resolve the thorny issue of slavery. I have not been dissuaded by the gigantic and continuous amount of bullshit that he was our nation's secular saint but merely the most malignant politician/attorney that could ever be put into the presidency, sufficient to disqualify him from such a lefty pinnacle.

In all the world's literature, there are 17,000 books on Abraham Lincoln (second spot only to the Bible), each author trying to outdo the others in praising the man. This adoration-of-Lincoln, or kiss-ass, industry is alive and well even after 150 years after his death! They perpetuate the saintly image of log cabin birth, of boot-strap elevation to prominence, and of saving the nation from the South. They all regurgitate the party line, suspending critical analysis, failing to see the pyrrhic victory over the South. No one questions, "What price, Union?" or "What price, emancipation?" The cream of America… one million dead! The son of a bitch should be vilified for what he did is a crime by any moral standards!

MOST TRAGIC ERA

That portion of history leading up to and including the Civil War (War between the States, War of Northern Aggression, War between Brothers, Lincoln's Madness) must be described by any and all historians as the stupidest era of American history. Stupidest because man allowed his basest, animal passions to rule over his better nature in addressing a long-standing problem of "a peculiar institution." Had it been addressed rationally in a calm, cerebral manner, the nation would have been spared the agony that followed. More than one million Americans perished in this stupid war!

My amazement as an impartial observer (from Canada) verges on the almost fatalistic, unquestioning acceptance by all Americans of this carnage as a necessary, unstoppable evolution of events seemingly beyond human control and reaching an inexorable conclusion. No one seemed responsible for this calamity! Even Abraham Lincoln in his second inaugural address said, "And the war came," as if it floated down from the air much as the plague. Thus, he evaded responsibility.

Knowing full well the hot-blooded nature of the Southern mind and afraid of losing face, he could not back down when the issue of resupplying Fort Sumter arose. By doing so, he jabbed a sharp stick in the South's eye and got a predictable response, and just as children in a school-yard altercation, he could plausibly exclaim, "But teacher, he hit me first," when they fired on the Fort!

The issue of slavery, a minor episode in the greater context and scope of human history, was deliberately exaggerated and magnified as a major confrontational issue falsely claiming it to be a sin where no biblical support exists for such a bald-faced lie if anyone cares to read that august tome. That it was nobly inspired to deal with that anomaly slavery much as drunks in a barroom brawl charges and countercharges were hurled until violence finally erupted to settle the issue once and for all. And it was, most tragically! Because they portrayed God's word as clearly against slavery, the abolitionists put enormous psychological pressure on all obedient Christians, making them believe they should observe the word of God and be against slavery too. Thus, the American Civil

War is clearly the worst case of fratricide in American and, perhaps, world history!

There has been, in recent years, finally, the seemingly grudging admission that the American Civil War was one of the world's greatest tragedies. Authors discuss ad nauseum the causes, objectives, and outcome without confronting the most serious aspect of the war: the butchery of about one million Americans to "solve" the thorny issue of slavery! It was of minor concern to them in the pursuit of a noble enterprise—the abolition of slavery—that so much blood was spilled. Despite their glossing over much of the unpleasantries, these facts remain: more people were killed or wounded in the Civil War than in *all* American wars combined; it was "the bloodiest war of the nineteenth century"; that "almost all families suffered some sort of casualty"; it "divided citizens, even families"; and it "left a bitter legacy that has never fully healed." All these facts should leave the readers astounded, amazed, and dumbfounded. Yet we go along with our lives as if the Civil War was merely a minor episode in our nation's history!

No matter how hard we look in our history books, there can be found *no* suggestion of an alternative, other than war, to persuade the South to give up slavery. Time after time we are told this was the only possible way to solve the dilemma of slavery in a democracy. Balderdash! If there could be found a historian with a critical eye with backbone and the temerity to utter the contrarian view, that Lincoln's high-handed, belligerent approach, though seemingly from the moral high ground, was wrong, wrong, wrong, then we could have a dialogue worthy of historical interest. For it becomes clearly apparent that Abraham Lincoln was totally lacking in diplomatic skills, of compromise, of negotiation, of give and take, of being satisfied with a half a loaf in dealing with this thorny issue of slavery. It was his way or the highway (to use the take it or leave it modern vernacular). He and his cohorts in crime, for the butchery of so many young people, was most certainly that began from the premise that slavery was an abomination or even a sin in the eyes of God. Without a supporting corollary to complete the syllogism, they leap to the conclusion: it must be abolished and abolished forthwith!

UNCONSCIONABLE COST OF THE AMERICAN CIVIL WAR

The only way to put even a dent in the rock-solid reputation of Abraham Lincoln and be the iconoclast of iconoclasts is to reveal the falsity of his reputation based upon unassailable facts. Sycophants and bullshitters of the Lincoln legacy have burnished an image of a secular saint who "saved" America by his firm leadership in the face of difficult opposition within and without the North. Yet in all my readings, no one has had the temerity and honesty to analyze that war without preconceived opinions presented to us by biased politicians and historians who wanted to hide from us the unconscionable and horrendous loss of human lives wasted over a minor issue: that of slavery!

In most of my readings about the American Civil War, the number of casualties reported seems elusive and inconsistent. To my amazement and consternation, the January 30–February 6, 2006, issue of the *U.S. News and World Report* indicated the losses for the Union were 646,392 and for the Confederacy 335,524. This loss of over one million Americans seems nowhere to be received with the horror and sadness that one would ordinarily expect from normal human beings. We are also told that the cost of this war was $5.2 billion, equivalent to 62 billion in 2002 currency. To put this all in perspective, the number of Americans killed during the Civil War exceeds the number killed in *all* of American wars *combined*!

DEATHS			COST 2billion	MIA
	Revolutionary War	3,977		
	War of 1812	2,260		
	Mexican War	13,283		
	Spanish-American War	2,446		
	World War I	116,516	191 "	
	World War II	295,000 (405,000)	2,896 "	78,000
	Korean War	36,642	336 "	8,192
	Vietnam War	58,193	494 "	2,646
	Persian Gulf War	382	76 "	1
	Kosovo	?	?	
	Afghanistan	3,931	?	4
	Iraq	? and counting	?	

ONE MILLION DEAD!

One million Americans died yet there is not one peep out of the historians expressing outrage, concern, sadness, or any negative emotion about this unconscionable and tremendous loss of life and effusion of blood! The greatest crime of the nineteenth century, the American Civil War, was followed by the greatest criminal cover-up and sanitization, beginning with Lincoln's cabinet, by the hypocritical abolitionists, and their blaspheming Quaker brethren and, finally, by the kiss-ass historians' gullibility and lack of critical analysis. Even now, in the twenty-first century, Lincoln is described as one of our greatest presidents. Bullshit! He should instead be categorized amongst the most brutal, bloodthirsty rulers of all time—Genghis Khan, Adolf Hitler, Joseph Stalin, Pol Pot, etc.—leaders who exhibited mindless brutality, who sacrificed (and wasted) countless members of their own people in a needless war, one that should have been averted by members of exemplary leadership. One million American lives were sacrificed to the greater good(?) of emancipating four million slaves, hardly a heroic and laudable deed.

In the long run, many logically felt there would be a gradual abolition of slavery, and this might require the nation to compensate the slave owners for their lost private property, much as the British had done with their slave owners. But this would require political leadership of exceptional patience and negotiating skills to accomplish this herculean, but delicate, task. Unfortunately, Abraham Lincoln was not that man!

DEMURRAL

It is not my view to support the institution of slavery nor to support the abolitionists in their militant quest for its eradication. Whether we regard it as a hideous exploitation, whether we regard it as a denial of basic human rights and democratic principles, or whether, as the Southerners insist, it has salutary and beneficial features. My concern and major focus is that once the decision to abolish is made, how best is it to be achieved? Abraham Lincoln's way of military force and brutal butchery was not the way! His way required little cerebration—only mindless brute force.

DISHONEST HISTORY

Much has been written, and continues to be written and rewritten, about the American Civil War. One needs only to look at the profusion of books written about Lincoln and the Civil War, second only to the number of books regarding the Bible, to realize there exists a Civil War writing industry in America. And they are all lies! The American Civil War was not a noble enterprise conducted by noble people for a noble purpose: the abolition of slavery! It was, moreover unbridled butchery on a gargantuan scale conducted by atavistic cretins intent on imposing their wills upon the nation. And their leader was Abraham Lincoln, a barroom, backwoods brawler of limited education, a lawyer/politician (not a statesman) who bamboozled America to embark on a murderous campaign to subdue the South to his iron will.

DIFFERENCES

The institution of slavery in the Southern states had a greater and more profound effect on the mentality of the people there than was realized by themselves and the people of the North. While loyal to the concept of maintaining Union with the North, they wished to preserve their peculiar institutions, ancient customs, and well-loved ways of life and thought. This philosophic romanticism, whose concepts of idealism, heroism, chivalry, sentiment, and love prevailed (as shown in the introduction of the movie "Gone with the Wind") and took hold on the minds of the aristocratic South, giving thoughts of a superior culture, of well-bred gentlemen, of refinement and leisure, of savoir faire, in distinct opposition to the coarse and materialistic North.

They were, in essence and fact, two separate and distinct worlds held together by ancient and traditional bonds, now fraying and weakened by repeated and progressively more violent frictions with the North.

MANDATE?

In the election of 1860, Abraham Lincoln received 1.8 million votes and the other three candidates received 2.8 million popular votes. Therefore, this plurality vote (39.1%) hardly constitutes a mandate from the general population to embark upon such a murderous campaign as the American Civil War. (I recognize he received a majority of the electoral votes, 180 to 72 for Breckenridge, 29 for Bell, and 12 for Douglas, but I insist the popular vote was a more accurate feeling of the general population!) A record-breaking 82% voted on November 6, 1860, and again I emphasize he did not get a majority of the popular vote. Even his birth state of Kentucky gave him a paltry 1,364 of its 167,223 votes!

APOCALYPSE AND ARMAGEDDON

The description of the American Civil War as a cataclysmic event in which "the powers of evil are totally destroyed, ushering in the eternal kingdom of God" qualifies it to be categorized as an apocalyptic event, or "the place where the final and conclusive battle between good and evil" or "the battle of that great day of God Almighty" qualifies it as Armageddon. Either definition suffices to imply an event of gargantuan proportions with enormous loss of life, a tidal wave of blood, and with great misery and woe. It has been, most certainly, the greatest catastrophe in American affairs! The faithful, convinced that the war was a noble and righteous crusade, allowed it to lurch from one gory, murderous, and exsanguinating battle to another and another and another, depleting the nation of its manhood.

The recent revelation that over one million Americans (North and South) had to be sacrificed in order to free four million slaves indicates that history books, and historians have lied to us when they sugarcoated and massaged the numbers as minor and insignificant.

The study of the life and times of Abraham Lincoln proves the inadvisability of electing a novice, a person with no previous executive (governmental) experience into the presidency. Despite all the accolades heaped upon this man for "saving" America, I like to use and paraphrase George Bernard Shaw's line: "What price Salvation?" and "What price Emancipation?" Except for myself, everyone seems to be saying that the deaths of over one million Americans (North and South) in order to free four million slaves was justified and of minor significance?!

Just as the thirteen colonies were in rebellion against the domineering mother country so too were the Southern states in rebellion against the domineering North. The principles of personal freedom and personal liberty identical in both instances and were articulated in the Declaration of Independence, Phases I and II, "When in the course of human events." The original Declaration did, and still does, command respect and obedience to the principles of personal liberty, therefore, when articulated by the South, it should command the same reverence and respect as the original! They are exactly the same! Only the timing is different!

DECLARATION

When Kosovo declared independence from Serbia on February 17, 2008, the United States quickly recognized it, and by February 21, a crowd of Serbs attacked the U.S. Embassy in Belgrade. Historically, when the South declared its independence from the North, Washington, (Abraham Lincoln and his war cabinet) angered by the South's impertinence, refused such a request and waged war upon them to keep them safely within the Union. Despite America's break from the oppression by the mother country, based upon philosophical concepts of individual liberty and individual freedom, Abraham Lincoln and his cabinet could not extend these self-same courtesies to the South. The Americans achieved their liberty from the oppressive British; the Kosovars got theirs from the Serbs.

THE SEEMINGLY UNRECOGNIZED HORROR OF THE CIVIL WAR

Much as man becomes hardened to the activities of a slaughterhouse so too do the veterans of the American Civil War seem to have become inured to the stench of the dead and dying resulting from the numerous battles. For example, Ulysses S. Grant, in his memoirs, recounts the battle of Shiloh (Pittsburgh Landing) with such dispassionate, clear, and precise prose, as to impart to the reader a coldness and callousness of a butcher in a slaughterhouse going about his business in an almost cavalier attitude. In a matter-of-fact manner he tells us:

> "Shiloh was the severest battle fought at the West during the war, and but few in the East equaled it for hard, determined fighting. I saw an open field, in our possession on the second day, over which the Confederates had made repeated charges the day before, so covered with dead that it would have been possible to walk across the clearing, in any direction, stepping on dead bodies, without a foot touching the ground."

He relates the episode as if the field of battle was covered merely by thousands of Persian rugs to keep him from treading on terra firma and not the thousands of human corpses… a ghastly sight. We recoil in horror at the image, but he does not. For him it happens every day, and he is used to it!

In his description of the battle of Champion Hill, we find a glimpse of humanity, but the callousness of a seasoned veteran dominates. Business as usual is the message we receive, and the business of the military is the killing business:

> "While a battle is raging one can see his enemy mowed down by the thousand, or the ten thousand, with great composure; but after the battle these scenes are distressing, and one is naturally disposed to do as much to alleviate the sufferings of an enemy as a friend…"

Has anyone but myself noticed that none of Mathew Brady's photographs of the battlefields reflects the true carnage that occurred there? Almost all of his prints show fewer than a dozen bodies strewn upon the ground! What kind of censorship and media control is this? I feel pictures of the dead by the thousands would have overwhelmed the grieving nation and perhaps impelled the populace to shorten Lincoln's presidency.

CRYSTAL BALL SPECULATIONS AND PREMISES

Apart from the issue and prominence of slavery as the precipitating cause of the Civil War, the argument goes that if the South had been allowed to secede from the Union, United States of America would have suffered a most calamitous collapse and disintegration. The novel experiment of "democracy" would have been an abject failure. Thus, "Save the Union" became the rallying cry urging the North to act forcefully and prevent such a catastrophe! My speculation, on the contrary, has equal merit. It is that had the South been allowed to go their own separate way, they would have both succeeded and prospered in their own ways: the North as capitalistic and industrial and the South as aristocratic and agrarian. Because of the already well-established commercial ties, trade between these two parts of the country would still occur. Investment opportunities in the South by either the North or Britain would help the South in an industrial renaissance. Synergistic harmonies between the two would assist both halves to prosper, much as Canada has a symbiotic relationship with America.

With regards to the Fugitive Slave Law, the North would no longer be obliged to return the escaped slaves to their slave owners. The safe haven for escaped slaves would no longer be the Canadian border but now the Mason-Dixon line and/or the Ohio River. *Why* was it primarily in America (and Britain) that slavery took on the appearance of sinful activity? The Bible does not support such an assertion, for in those days the practice of slavery was viewed as a common everyday occurrence.

Why was it only in America that the "solution" to the problem of slavery required so much effusion of blood? South America and the Caribbean had millions more slaves and heir resolution was relatively bloodless and peaceful. Are we to conclude that *we* are the volatile and "hot-blooded" people of the western world?

IMPACT OF THE CIVIL WAR ON AMERICA IN THE AFTERMATH

Author Virginia Nicholson in her study "Singled Out: How Two Million Women Survived Without Men after the First World War" tells us of the enormous impact the war had on the lives of women in Great Britain after this French holocaust. She discusses this "lost generation," euphemistically known as "surplus women"—1.75 million spinsters stranded when an equivalent number of their boys were tragically slaughtered and buried in France. It was so bad that she quotes a headmistress telling her pupils: "Only one in ten of you girls can ever hope to marry. You will have to make your way in the world as best you can," for she was following the age-old tradition that marriage and motherhood were what women had always been for.

In America, after the tragic episode known as the Civil War, historians, economists, and sociologists all have failed to study and write on the enormous impact the deaths of over 600,000 Americans (North and South) had on the women left behind.

When the nightmare known as the American Civil War ended, at least a small minority of historians might pause to reconsider, to spend some time in self-examination as to the justification for that carnage, especially because of the inordinate number of deaths squandered in pursuit of the Holy Grail of 1861. No one of any stature dared conclude it was a military and moral catastrophe of historical proportions; instead they all followed the party line that it was a noble crusade for a noble purpose sought by noble people, and take your pick to end slavery and/or to preserve the Union.

Abraham Lincoln pursued the war with passion and single-mindedness and ferocity that belied his calm exterior. His messianic impulses possessed his whole being: the South must be brought into the fold even if he had to kill every and each Southerner to do so! He eschewed moral suasion in favor of the no-brainer: military conquest! It is because of the arrogance and temerity of historians, who insist in telling us that history is what they say it is, that impels me to be contrarian and question their assumptions and presentations.

I am exceedingly tired of all the bullshit the "historians" have foisted upon us for all these generations of how wonderful a president was Abraham Lincoln. Despite all the favorable rhetoric, the facts speak for themselves and disprove all these lies if only a contrarian will point them out to all those who have been misled and seduced by the clever presentations. The American Civil War was nothing but a brutal family feud on a monumental scale where American fought American, and all because a determined president failed miserably with the arduous task of negotiation, of compromise, of give and take, instead plunged us wildly into an unnecessary war, where over a million casualties resulted and an expenditure of over $5.2 billion! It seems apparent that the historians, almost without exception, have formed a universal, incestuous fraternity of idolatrous worshippers ready to defend to the death the received spotless bullshit of Abraham Lincoln's life.

I am inclined to agree with George Templeton Strong, described as a diarist, who reacted thusly when he heard of the Republican nomination of one term Illinois Congressman Abraham Lincoln. "He cut a great many rails, and worked on a flatboat in early youth; all which is somehow presumptive evidence of his statesmanship."

For those who believe that only "characters preeminent for ability and virtue" should achieve the presidency, as Alexander Hamilton did, Lincoln was not that character. He proved, as Martin Van Buren did, that intrigue and the art of popularity would suffice. Lincoln's handlers at the Chicago Convention, with their behind-the-scenes machinations, proved this in spades!

DAMN THE HISTORIANS

When I read all the historians' accounts of the American Civil War, I see a herd of lemmings rushing to worship at the shrine of Abraham Lincoln; I see a herd of sheep mindlessly following the Judas Goat. Both metaphors show us how the historians have followed, without question, without skepticism, without criticism, without any challenge, the accounts that were laid down on day one. They gush with ecstasy and admiration for he "saved the Union" and "freed the slaves." No one dares ask "What price Union?" "What price emancipation?"

How can they overlook the mountain of corpses piled like a huge landfill-to-the-sky that should temper their enthusiasm for the man? How can they avert their eyes to this carnage of 1,000,000!) casualties? An excessive and exorbitant price!

How can they plug up their noses from the overwhelming stench from the thousands of decomposing bodies?

How can they plug up their ears to the agonizing cries and moans of the wounded and dying?

Over 1,000,000 casualties just to free 4 million slaves! Damn them all to hell for aiding and abetting in this horrible crime of the millennium and for its subsequent clever cover-up!

HISTORY

HISTORIANS AND HISTORY

In perhaps one of his smallest books, the noted historian Arthur M Schlesinger Jr., *The Disuniting of America*, ruminates about his profession, while defending its performance admits it's less than ideal presentation. He begins by saying, "Historians do their damnedest (Is he trying to convey to us that historians are heroes on a crusade?) to maintain the standards of their trade. Heaven knows how dismally we fall short of our ideals, how sadly our interpretations are dominated and distorted by unconscious preconceptions, how obsessions of race and nation blind us to our own bias. We remain creatures of our times, prisoners of our own experience, swayed hither and yon, like sinful mortals, by partisanship, prejudice, dogma, by fear and by hope."

Two paragraphs later he goes on, "Historians must always strive toward the unattainable ideal of objectivity. But as we respond to contemporary urgencies, we sometimes exploit the past for nonhistorical purposes, taking from the past, or projecting upon it, what suits our own society or ideology. History, thus, manipulated becomes an instrument less of disinterested intellectual inquiry than of social cohesion and political purpose.

"People live by their myths, and some may argue that the facts can be justifiably embroidered if embroidement serves a higher good, such as the nurture of a nation or the elevation of a race. It may seem more important to maintain a beneficial fiction than to keep history pure, especially when there is no such thing as sure history anyway. This may have been that Plato had in mind when he proposed the idea of the 'noble lie' in the Republic."

The above three paragraphs show a historian striving mightily to put an honest face on historians' works, ruminating philosophically on the ideas and ideals of his craft, but sufficiently vague as to cause confusion in the readers' minds. Without concrete references to illustrate his meaning of how history was corrupted for social and/or political purposes, one leaves us to our own devices to imagine them. Is it not within the historian's distinct purview to not only write about historical facts but also explain them in the context of underlying currents in society? Why did Schlesinger not do so?

The triggering effect these three paragraphs had on me was to conclude that all of the events surrounding the Civil War were prostituted by historians for the "interests of social cohesion and political purposes" or to "serve a higher good, such as the nurture of a nation or the elevation of a race." These oblique references by such an illustrious historian made me conclude he was thinking about the "history" of the Civil War, a history that was so sanitized from the original events as to be unrecognizable. An undisputed feature of wars is that it was written by the winning side, and it is through their eyes, and their eyes only, that we come to "understand" its historical importance, for contrary opinions as any student will tell you, are virtually nonexistent. Why is this so? Does not Orwell's analysis resonate here? "Who controls the past, controls the future?" "Who controls the present, controls the past." It was the original historians and politicians who wrote down *their* views as to what occurred during the Civil War, i.e., were "in control of the past" and, therefore, it was they who "controlled the future." Today, the politically correct descendants regurgitate as *they* "control the present" to perpetuate the original history, i.e., "control the past," the great undisputed lie that still goes unexamined!

Therefore it becomes incumbent upon the reader to not merely have an open mind but also one that is critical and aware of historians' biases as well as honest mistakes even if they have tried their "damnedest" to be honest, fair, and accurate. We must be wary of the historians' intent: is it really history or is it propaganda? Are the factual inaccuracies or deliberate lies designed to persuade or convince? Is it presenting the historian's personal point of view—a perspective of "political correctness" to justify events for a noble cause? Is it justifiable? Or are they "smelly little orthodoxies contending for our souls?" How can we reconcile the need for collective action to remedy society's ills, thereby surrendering to the state the power over personal freedoms?

Arthur Schlesinger Jr., puts it more elegantly by stating, "The purpose of history is to promote not self-esteem, but understanding of the world and the past, dispassionate analysis, Judgment, and perspective, respect for divergent cultures and traditions, and unflinching protection for those unifying ideas of tolerance, democracy, and human rights that make free historical enquiry possible."

ANOTHER COVER-UP

In an otherwise excellent historical analysis, *The Disuniting of America*, by Arthur Schlesinger Jr., I take issue with his characterization of the abolition of slavery, as all the historians seem to do, as a noble accomplishment. He asserts, or even brags about, the superiority of American traditions that no matter what its flaws, corrections were always made to rectify the errors. He states, "The crimes of the West have produced their own antidotes. They have provoked great movements to end slavery, to raise the status of women, to abolish torture, to combat racism, to defend freedom of enquiry and expression, to advance personal liberty and human rights."

It is here that I take exception with his inclusion of the abolition of slavery, the greatest and bloodiest carnage of American history, with all the other civil rights struggles, which were in stark contrast pacifistic and, therefore, bloodless. As with all the other historians before him, Schlesinger follows the party line in portraying the Civil War as a minor episode in the flow of American history—a minor bump in the road that needs little no attention by the American populace. I, on the other hand, view it as a major 9.5-on-the-Richter scale earthquake, obliterating the road and causing the bus carrying American historical traditions to careen wildly and crash into the ditch, killing many and wrecking the bus so badly as to retard its forward progress for years to come.

Nowhere but in America was the abolition of slavery associated with so much killing as it lurched along to a violent denouement and solution. The Age of Enlightenment, a time of celebration of the powers of human reason, seemed to bypass America and left us still mired in the Dark Ages, where ignorance and barbarism prevailed in a Hatfield-McCoy style of family feud. Insults resulted in reactions, reactions brought about counterreactions, back and forth, ever escalating with greater and greater vehemence, and the mounds of corpses piled ever and ever higher, yet the historians seem not to notice.

HISTORY?

Voltaire's acerbic assessment of history was that it "is nothing more than a picture of crimes and misfortunes." Insisting that only philosophers should write history, he went on to explain: "In all nations, history is disfigured by fable, till at last philosophy comes to enlighten man; and when it does finally arrive in the midst of this darkness, it finds the human mind so blinded by centuries of error, that it can hardly undeceive it; it finds facts, ceremonies and monuments heaped up to prove lies." He also sometimes referred to history as "the Mississippi of falsehoods." Later he went on to conclude that "History is after all nothing but a pack of tricks which we play upon the dead… history proves that anything can be proved by history."

It is fallacious to assume that history is merely the transmission of a certain body of settled knowledge. The inquiring mind, considering that history may be wrong, should question the absoluteness of the established "history" and painstakingly arrive at their own interpretation of events.

HISTORIANS

Eric Hoffer, "the primitive philosopher," once made an observation on philosophers, which I find equally applicable to historians. He said, "There are quite a number of people who have a vested interest in the stuff, make a noble living out of it, and they conspire with one another to keep it alive." Those compassionate instigators, who precipitated the American Civil war, created an aura around Abraham Lincoln—that the War was a noble crusade, that he was a noble leader who freed the slaves and saved the Union and that the butchery of over 1,000,000 Americans was justifiable homicide! Generations of historians, programmed at the shrine of Saint Abraham, have assiduously perpetuated this bullshit to subsequent generations! In reality, the American Civil War was nothing but a continuous and never-ending chain of battles characterized by unparalleled slaughter of grotesque ferocity disproportionate to the stakes involved!

HISTORY

History should always be suspect because it typically reflects the interests and preferences of those in power. Once lies have been repeated enough times it acquires the patina of truthfulness, especially to noninquiring minds. In "On Liberty," John Stuart Mill insists that knowledge not meeting the test of repeated challenge is not knowledge. Someone else also echoed this sentiment by saying: "The unexamined life is not worth living." I dismiss the received wisdom not merely by contrary evidence and argument but also impugning the motives of those who established it. The bodies of over *1,000,000* Americans buried in graves in enormous cemeteries is the evidence contradicting the viewpoints that the American Civil War was a noble and heroic enterprise and worth the price paid to establish the freedom and liberty of 4 million slaves. Bullshit!

HISTORY

A study of the past to serve the higher purpose of distinguishing right decisions from wrong help avoid making the same mistake twice. Also to get the facts straight.

MISCELLANEOUS

(History… bunk) Perhaps my perspective might be equated to the description by Richard Gordon in his book, *The Alarming History of Medicine*, about that famous physician Thomas Sydenham (1624–1689) "He enjoyed the admirable Cromwellian quality of sniffing the whiff of bullshit in the winds of history."

HIGH ROAD?

In a letters column of the Investor's Business Daily, the writer, David Tempest, of Venice, California, presents a philosophical view that exactly epitomizes how I feel about the Civil War. He says, "Human beings have basically two sides to our nature. One is an enlightened aspect, where we display wisdom, tolerance, compassion, humanity and anger toward injustice. The other aspect prevalent in society manifests itself as ignorance, arrogance and greed—where we resort to violence to try to solve the problems that confront us and are quick to categorize people in order to demonize them, not realizing that as human beings they are fundamentally just like us. In a crisis… the question is: Do we follow the higher path or do we resort to violence simply because it is the easier route? Injustices are perpetrated all over the world every day. Let's stand against injustice everywhere and fight it using education, cooperation, reconciliation, dialogue and the rule of law that constitutes hundreds of years of our highest wisdom. Let's Choose the difficult path and reform ourselves. Only by manifesting our greater selves can we hope to solve the problems in our own backyard and around the world."

NEGOTIATION VERSUS WAR

Before he became an ardent abolitionist, Reverend Theodore Parker on June 7, 1846, in a speech at the Melodeon, decried America's war with Mexico: "I maintain that aggressive war is a sin; that it is a national infidelity, a denial of Christianity and of God… Treason against the people, against mankind, against God, is a great sin, not lightly to be spoken of. The political authors of the war on this continent, and at this day, are either utterly incapable of statesman's work, or else guilty of that sin. Fools they are, or traitors they must be. How tamely the people yield their necks—and say 'Take our sons for the war—we care not, right or wrong.'"

However, when the American Civil War broke out in 1861 he seems to have forgotten this speech as he advocated support for Lincoln's war against the South, despite the fact that the leadership "are either incapable of statesman's work, or else guilty of that sin." How tamely the people yield their necks and say, "Take our sons for the war—we care not, right or wrong."

THE FICTION THAT IS LINCOLN

The countless writers on the life and times of Abraham Lincoln seem to have strayed far and wide from their professional responsibilities as historians, i.e., to present events in an impersonal and objective manner. Instead, as fervent fanatics with a herd mentality, they have allowed their feelings to color their thinking as they embellish his fame. As acolytes they can be found worshipping at and tending to the eternal flame at the shrine of Abraham Lincoln jealously guarding the party line from all intruders and from all common sense. They forever praise Lincoln for "preserving the Union," portraying it in heroic terms as if it were the Holy Grail!

Time after time, writer after writer, all seem intent in outdoing the others in their praising of the man but obviously suspending critical judgment as they elevate him in the pantheon of American heroes and saints. Conveniently, they forget that he was a clever successful attorney who spent most of his adult life as a career politician either running for or serving in office, factors which together should disqualify him from saintly consideration.

The crowning insult to my intelligence is the metaphysical injections in their writings comparing him to Jesus Christ! For just as Jesus was considered as the "redeemer of mankind" so too was Lincoln ascribed as the "redeemer president" for "saving" the United States through his intercessions. This assertion verges on the preposterous for instead of sacrificing himself for America, he brutally wasted his countrymen to the tune of 1,000,000 brave souls! Redeemer president indeed!

As one gets older and reads differing accounts on similar historical matters, it becomes evident that many historians conveniently present only the favorable aspects when discussing their heroes and slant their stories with evasions, distortions, and even outright lies. And so it is with Abraham Lincoln whom the American historians have elevated to a status of secular saint. One of the nation's saddest moments occurred on December 26, 1862, with the mass execution (hanging) of thirty-eight Sioux Indians by the direct order of Abraham Lincoln. Of course his supporters will vehemently argue that the president had no choice but to order this execution, but such a callous decision is incompatible with an image of a compassionate secular saint, as they would have us believe, and more in keeping with that of a brutal unfeeling tyrant! What a grisly sight it must have been!

Horace Greeley—perhaps unduly influenced by his "radical" managing editor, Charles Dana, he at first supported the suppression of South's efforts at independence, but later, when the death toll of first Bull Run made him recoil in horror, he favored conciliation. It is often remembered that he advocated "Go west, young man, go west," he also advocated "Let the erring sisters depart in peace," i.e., recommending that the South be allowed to establish the Confederate States of America and go their own way.

It is said Horace Greeley suffered a "nervous breakdown," yet throughout the slaughter of the Civil War and all its attendant horrors, he is one of the few who had the common sense to try to stop the war and to try to stop the unnecessary effusion of brotherly blood! Unfortunately, the war machine was in control by an intense war cabinet intent on victory, whatever the cost

As a nonhistorian I am, therefore, not bound by any conventions that restrict my inquiry into questions of what has been previously written as "gospel truth." In the pantheon of dictators, butchers, and just plain leaders, who have caused the unnecessary and needless deaths of thousands upon thousands of young men and created such destruction as a pestilential plague then, in that list, we must include that of Abraham Lincoln. Through his monomaniacal pursuit of the "erring sisters," he and his radical cabinet would push their agenda to the ultimate extreme of annihilating everyone opposed to their viewpoint.

It has been said that the essence of totalitarianism is a political order that recognizes no higher authority, no limits, and no decencies and, according to this definition, the brutal reign of Abraham Lincoln clearly places him in that pantheon of great dictators as such as Adolf Hitler, Joseph Stalin, Pol Pot, etc.

ABRAHAM LINCOLN AND SAINTHOOD

From years of experience and the study of many history books, it seems an observed fact that the longer a person is dead and buried, the greater is his/her reputation. A case in point is the life of Abraham Lincoln. Having already achieved an exalted status in life then, cut down in his prime by an evil assassin's bullet, his reputation has been further embellished by hordes of ovine sycophantic historians eager to enhance their image as acolytes to a famous secular saint. No man in American history has achieved such an exalted status in a profusion of so many books of so much worshipful adoration.

Only secular heretics or the most obtuse of politically incorrect would deny his exalted status as the "savior of the nation." For over 150 years we have been bombarded by the perpetual idolatrous mythmaking of Abraham Lincoln by hordes of obsequious historians who slavishly follow the party line. If not miracles then the "good works" of saving the Union and freeing the slaves, alone or together, qualify him for elevation to the exalted status of saint. But conveniently lost in the rush to genuflect at his altar is the fact that, in his monomaniacal pursuit of a genocidal policy of subduing the South, and the arrogance and vision of his moral superiority, he ultimately caused, and is responsible for, the deaths of over 1,000,000 Americans. On this alone he merits the opprobrium of a mindless bloodthirsty butcher!

In the realm of propaganda coups, I am in a quandary trying to decide between two world-class productions occurring consecutively in the mid-1800s. The first, undoubtedly a blue-ribbon prize winner in the annals of world propaganda, would be Harriet Beecher Stowe's *Uncle Tom's Cabin*. To this very day this seemingly innocuous maudlin production still resonates in the minds of not only Americans but also of peoples worldwide. Upon meeting her in the White House, Abraham Lincoln is quoted as saying: "So this is the little lady who wrote that book that made this great war," and in doing so testifies to the enormous impact her work had upon the American psyche. Undoubtedly, the second world's greatest propaganda coup is a two-parter: (a) the portrayal of the American Civil War as a noble crusade to emancipate the Negro slave, and (b) the portrayal and characterization of Abraham Lincoln as the benevolent President who led the Union forces and "saved the Union." According to the long line of bullshitting historians, he acted to preclude the South from destroying the Union and that noble experiment in democracy through their declaration of independence from the North. His crystal ball predicted this calamitous outcome, whereas mine, equally valid, would have predicted that

HOLY GRAIL

In Christian legend it was (1) the cup that Jesus Christ drank from at the Last Supper or (2) Joseph of Aramethia, a follower of Christ used the cup to capture blood flowing from Jesus's wounds. Later he was imprisoned and the grail mysteriously appeared and fed him. After his release, he used the cup for communion services. Later the phrase came to refer to the pursuit of any esteemed object attained by long endeavor.

Lincoln's "Holy Grail" was his obsession with preserving the Union. His greatest fear was that if the South should successfully secede, the democratic experiment would fail and the North would collapse. By cleverly focusing the nation's attention on this pursuit (and minimizing the importance of the slavery issue) he marshaled the nation's energies to dealing with the South. Fiercely determined to preserve the Union, he miscalculated the cost and duration to achieve it. As compromise was not in his nature, waging war as absolute dictator was his answer. *He pursued this vision with such real and passion, with the total exclusion of reason, that the inevitable slaughter of over 1,000,000 Americans. North and South resulted!*

Much as a stern father disciplines disobedient children wishing to grow up and go out on their own (self-determination). Lincoln dealt with the South by taking them out to the woodshed, not to beat them, but instead to kill most of them and beating the rest to an inch of their lives!

INTERESTING COMMENTS BY SOME NOTABLES

When I read a comment by Cyril Connolly: "In spite of the slow conversion of progressive ideas into the fact of history, the Dark Ages have a way of coming back. Civilization—the world of affection and reason and freedom and justice—is a luxury which must be fought for," I am reminded of the of the American Civil War.

The commandment "Thou shalt not kill" clearly indicates that violence is incompatible with the nature of God, and the nature, therefore, of the soul. The butchery of the American Civil War shows that supposed Christians, on both sides, seemed to have failed to follow this simple instruction.

George Bernard Shaw is often quoted as saying, "Peace is better than war, but infinitely more arduous."

Samuel Butler: "God cannot alter the past, but historians can."

I particularly like Sylvia Parkhurst's comment about war: "This war did not justify the sacrifice of a single mother's son," and I apply it to the American Civil War.

The ancient Greek historian Thucydedes warned, even then, of the tendency of historians "who are less interested in telling the truth than in catching the attention of the public, whose authorities cannot be checked, and whose subject-matter, owing to the passage of time, is mostly lost in the unreliable streams of mythology."

This horrific view of warfare was reflected in later years by Teddy Roosevelt as he was devastated by the death of his son Quentin in WW I in July 1818. His brutal analysis showed his despondency: "Death in battle was no more glorious than death in an abattoir."

In my humble estimation Peter Gomes, a Harvard chaplain, hit the nail right on the head, and his statement resonates with the historical representation of Abraham Lincoln's life: "Myth is more important than history. History is arbitrary, a collection of facts. Myths we choose, we create, we perpetuate." And so it was with the fantastic creations known as the life of Abraham Lincoln!

Another cynical view of history was made by Richard Reeves when he said, "A lot of history is just dirty politics cleaned up for the consumption of children and other innocents."

EVOLUTION OF THE DEMOCRATIC STATE

Perhaps from as far back as the caveman days when associations of people are founded on the family, where the father had absolute power over his wives and children, and especially, the family property, as these families became larger and more numerous, they formed associations of families and thereby created "states." Given the innate belligerency and will to dominate these often resulted from the conquest of one group of families over another and the leader of the victors became "king" The laws of this society did not originate in the "sovereignty" of the people but of necessity by the power of the father in this patriarchal group, as absolute monarch.

Then along came George Buchanan (b 1506) in Scotland who, one hundred years before Hobbes and 200 years before Rousseau, introduced the "social-contract" theory, a medieval doctrine that the sole source of political power, under God, is the people. Later in time this evolved to state that government is a covenant between God, the people and the king to obey and uphold the "true religion." Any king failing to do so may be deposed. On a lesser, secular scale, the government is a pact between king and people: the king to rule justly, the people to obey peaceably. The king is the instrument, not the dictator, of the law.

Thus, we see that before the origin of society, men lived like animals in the wild, free from all restraints but their physical limitations, recognizing no law and no private property and following instincts in seeking food and mates. To protect themselves from outside threats, men formed social organizations, delegating their collective authority to a chief or king but sovereignty remained in the people. In the Anglo-Saxon world, the Magna Carta may be regarded as a watershed document indicating the beginning of devolution of power from absolute monarchy to more power being invested in the people.

PHILOSOPHY AND DEMOCRACY

DEVOLUTION

The historical accounts regarding the Magna Carta was so eloquent for it was at Runnymede, England, in 1215, that this historic document, representing a watershed event in the political world, was signed. Frustrated and angered by King John's despotic rule, the barons forced him to sign this "constitutional" document in which was described a radical change in the relationship between ruler and ruled, and the propaganda (BS) of the Divine Right of Kings. Prior to this event, kings had the reputation of ruling as despots, rarely taking the advice of anyone and arbitrarily imposing their will upon the populace. Henceforth, their power was restrained, restricted, and circumscribed and eventually there evolved a system of government where the leaders governed their subjects by the *consent of the governed*, where each and every citizen had defined rights and responsibilities, clearly articulated in a constitution or a bill of rights. Step by step, the Petition of Right of 1628, the Bill of Rights of 1689 after the "Glorious Revolution," and the Toleration Acts of 1689, more and more power was taken from the king and put in the hands of Parliament and, therefore, the people!

Subsequent world-shaking events (revolutions), the American Revolution of 1776 that resulted in the Declaration of Independence and the Constitution, the French Revolution, and the Declaration of the Rights of Man and Citizen of 1789, all led to the increase in power of the ruled and decrease in arbitrary power of the ruler.

Such was not the case when the South revolted against the oppressive actions of the North. Here the progression of the rights of man toward liberty, freedom and self-determination came to a sudden catastrophic halt, and essential reversal, by the actions of a virtual dictator of uncompromising rigidity and uncommon brutality, Abraham Lincoln! It was he who denied the South their fundamental rights to self-determination (American Declaration of Independence, Phase II) by ruthlessly crushing their efforts at freedom from the domination of the more populous, industrial North. It was he whose carnage suppressed the desires of other oppressed peoples in the world to challenge entrenched power for years to come. It was he who caused the bitter internecine feud among brothers to the tune of 1,000,000 casualties. Were we to see a reincarnation, a dictatorial throwback of ancient Europe, of a bloody brute, a terrible tyrant wreaking havoc upon his own people in an exercise of cold-blooded iron will, exsanguinating the nation's manhood, North and South. Yet the carefully crafted propaganda persists declaring him of saintly qualities for "preserving" and "saving the Union."

NATURAL RIGHTS OF MAN

All throughout man's history, many ideas seem to percolate down through the ages only to resurface at some later date and be accorded the impression of newness and originality. In fact "The British Rights of Man" (1689), a document reflecting John Locke's (and others) profound photographical analysis of man's natural rights argumentation can be viewed as the ancestor and precursor to the Declaration of Independence (1776) and the French Declaration of the Rights of Man and the Citizen (1789). The basic utterances of all these documents insist that all rights are undeniable, indisputable inherent assets, which reside in the individual and, therefore, the people. These natural rights of man are always retained by, and cannot be separated from, the individual, and a direct corollary of this view would be freedom of association. Man has the *right* "not subject to any earthly power hut only his own consent" to associate with like-minded people of his own choosing, to pursue a course in life of his own liking, making at all times his own decisions that "he thinks fit for the preservation of himself" not being dictated to by others but perhaps only when he voluntarily surrenders this right.

Therefore, just as the American colonists, an amalgamation of like-minded peoples, declared their unhappiness and chose independence from the mother country Britain, so too did the Southern states have the right to unite with their "own people" and declare their independence from Mother Washington. They too declared a natural right to enter into an agreement with others having similar viewpoints to obtain a governing body more to their liking and break the bonds with an oppressive government led by Abraham Lincoln.

The lofty philosophical utterances of the American Declaration of Independence plus the writings of the French philosopher Jean Jacques Rousseau led the French to create the "Declaration of the Rights of Man and the Citizen," which was adopted by the National Assembly on August 17, 1789. This document, reflecting the French Enlightenment, adopted language rejecting absolute monarchy in favor of natural rights of man, self-determination in government, personal liberty under the rule of law, and fair taxation. All people were considered free and equal in "liberty, property, security and freedom from oppression."

From the 1689 bill Jefferson borrowed many of their philosophical ideals—trial by jury, right to bear arms, outlawing cruel and unusual punishment, excessive bail—but his greatest achievement was that "we are endowed by our Creator with certain inalienable rights… that among these are life, liberty and the pursuit of happiness." In this democracy that was, thus, created, ultimate authority resides not in the government but in that peoples constituting that nation.

It is worth noting in passing that Argentina declared independence from Spain in 1810 and Mexico in 1822. Also in 1822, Brazil threw off the Portuguese yoke.

Unfortunately, the two documents, the Declaration and the Constitution, contained within it profound and philosophical utterances so lofty and ideal as to clash noticeably with existing reality. And that reality was the prior existence and continuing presence of slavery with all its odious connotations. In a nation that boasted that "all men are created equal; that they are endowed by their Creator with certain inalienable Rights, that among these are Life, Liberty and the pursuit of Happiness," this declaration rings hollow.

In deference to the members from the South, any mention of the slave trade or of slavery was omitted from the document. It was a ticking time bomb left for later generations to deal with and to attempt to solve. Great was the explosion there from, i.e., the Civil War, the greatest disaster to ever befall America! In my humble opinion, had they addressed the issue of slavery in the Declaration of Independence, had they put any sort of restrictions upon it, the rock upon which the Southern economy was built, it would have created such an uproar as to bring about the South's refusal to support the North in their struggle to break free from Britain's domination. Any attempt to go it alone without the help of the South in their battle with Britain would have ended in abject failure and they would have been crushed in battle and the leaders hung unceremoniously.

History books characteristically portray the American Revolution in heroic terms, as a struggle of an oppressed people against the despotic rule of Great Britain, and who is determined to crush the hopes and aspirations of a young nation seeking its place in the world. "No taxation without representation" was the Americans' battle cry.

History books, on the other hand, portray the South in totally different terms even though the scenario is remarkably similar, i.e., where the South wanted to be free of oppressive Northern domination. Prior to the actual bloody battles the North waged clever psychological warfare upon the South vehemently attacking them as sinful and evil exploiters of Negro slaves. Unfortunately, the South had no effective countermeasures against this clever onslaught, especially against the most emotionally effective battle cries "rebellion (secession) is treason" or "the Union must be preserved"!

EVOLUTION OF REPRESENTATIVE (SELF-DETERMINATION) GOVERNMENT IN AMERICA

When the Virginia Company's (Jamestown) economy faltered, the angry shareholders instituted a series of reforms hoping to turn the venture into a profitable one. A major step in that direction was the replacement of the arbitrary law of the governor by English Common Law. In 1619, new management was brought in and Governor Yeardley summoned an *elected* legislative assembly, the House of Burgesses. Landowning males over seventeen years old were eligible to vote for two representatives from each private estate, and two from each of the company's four estates.

When rough seas forced the Mayflower to land at Cape Cod, they landed beyond their appointed bounds of the Virginia Company, and the "strangers" (non-Pilgrims) declared their freedom from any commands. The Pilgrims, viewing this as a threat of mutiny, composed a short of self-government, "civil body politic" to "frame just and equal laws." This document was signed by almost all the adult males, including forty-one of the Pilgrim Fathers. Thus, the Mayflower Compact is rightly considered the first written constitution in North America. (December 1620)

The original compact has since disappeared. The version below follows the spelling and punctuation given in the history *Of Plimoth Plantation*, written by William Bradford, second governor of Plymouth colony.

In ye name of God Amen. We whose names are underwritten, the loyall subjects of our dread soveraigne Lord King James, by ye grace of God, of Great Britaine, Franc, & Ireland king, defender of ye faith, &c. Haveing undertaken, for ye glorie of God, and advancement of ye Christian faith and honour of our king & countrie, a voyage to plant ye first colonie in ye Northerne parts of Virginia, doe by these presents solemnly & mutualy in ye presence of God, and one of another, covenant, & combine ourselves together into a Civil body politic; for our better ordering, & preservation & furtherance of ye ends aforesaid; and by virtue hereof to enact, constitute, and frame such just & equall

Lawes, ordinances, Acts, constitutions, & offices, from time to time, as shall be thought most meete & convenient for ye generall good of ye colonie: unto which we promise all due submission and obedience. In witnes whereof we have hereunder subscribed our names at Cap-Codd ye -11- of November, in ye year of ye raigne of our soveraigne Lord King James of England, France, & Ireland ye eighteenth, and of Scotland ye fiftie fourth. Ano Dom. 1620.

Thus, we see in the American colonies the germination of ideas that the citizens of a society could join freely and agree to govern themselves by making universally binding laws for the common good. Other colonial documents over the years have shown a progressive evolutionary process is the ideas of self-determination by its citizens. Among these are: the Fundamental Orders of Connecticut 1639, New England Articles of Confederation 1643, Maryland Toleration Act 1649, New Albony Plan of Union 1754, Resolutions of the Stamp Act Congress1765, First Continental Congress: Declaration of Colonial Rights 1774, Second Continental Congress: Declaration of the Causes and Necessity of Taking up Arms 1775, the Olive Branch Petition 1775, Virginia Declaration of Rights 1776, and most importantly, the Declaration of Independence, July 4, 1776!

DECLARATION

The lofty moral philosophical concepts of basic human rights, of human dignity, of universal aspirations such as life, liberty, and pursuit of happiness, as articulated in the Declaration of Independence, were the prime movers of American progress. We are driven to fulfill the great human desire to find commonality with like-minded individuals, i.e., the brotherhood of man. Natan Sharansky articulated precisely when he said, "The right to live a unique way of life is a right worth fighting for and, if necessary, worth dying for." The Declaration of Independence described all these issues as it attempted to defend the causes of friction between the colonies and the mother country.

Unfortunately, when this principle was resurrected by the South in their frictions with the North, this was rejected by the legalistic mind of Abraham Lincoln who insisted that, when the South signed on to be part of the United States, it was a "legal agreement" binding them forever. And Abraham Lincoln, as president, would enforce these terms even if he had to kill every Southerner to do so. Philosophy be damned! Thus, Abraham Lincoln's presidency represents the triumph of might over right, of totalitarian oppression over individual freedom. Rejecting any suggestions of protracted and laborious negotiations with the South over the issue of slavery, he preferred the "easy way" of military might believing he could easily crush the South and beat them into submission with his "ninety day recruits"! Quickly disabused of that notion with the punch in the nose at Manassas / Bull Run, he found himself on the slippery slope of an American Armageddon and with righteous indignation pursued a policy of retribution and vengeance worthy of the world's worst tyrants.

He most certainly trashed the profound philosophical utterances of the Declaration of Independence where the colonial "freedom fighters" succeeded with their concepts of individual self-determination. Not so with the Southern "freedom fighters"! What kind of leader makes war on his own people? In Lincoln's case, an iron-fisted backwoods, barroom brawler, a megalomaniac drunk with the power of the presidency, determined to impose his iron will upon the nation!

CONCEPT OF INDIVIDUAL FREEDOM

The preeminence of the Anglo-Protestant historical inheritance in America stems from the original new arrivals upon this continent either from those at Jamestown or from the Pilgrims on Cape Cod. It is from these seeds that the Anglo-Protestant system of values began and came to prevail with each subsequent and succeeding generation adopting these values. These are: rule of law, honoring of covenants, and emphasis on individual freedom. Some have said that the very way Westerners think about the human condition, through the intellectual disciplines of philosophy and history, stems from those of Ancient Greece. History tells us that these eventually took hold firmly in Great Britain, i.e., traditions of individual rights and responsibilities, minimal government, and a strong civil society. So we have come to appreciate that what we have in the New World was a transplantation and continuation of well-established philosophical traditions that had its origins in the "mother country."

In Ronald Reagan's famous speech in Westminster in 1982, he insisted on "man's instinctive desire for freedom and self-determination," and added, "it would be cultural condescension, or worse, to say that any people prefer dictatorship to democracy."

Here again, added to many other historical examples, we see these profundities clash with the enlightened dictatorship of Abraham Lincoln who arrogated the powers of government to "dictate" to the nation from his lofty Washington perspective what it must believe and what guidelines it must follow.

When the Convention of Virginia met to consider the question of secession, the slave-holding section of the state was somewhat startled by the logical but novel declaration of one of the western members, that the "right of revolution can be exercised as well by a portion of the citizens of the State against the State government, as it can be exercised by the whole people of a State against their Federal Government."

NATURAL RIGHTS

The government, with its organization and laws, has the major function of protecting the citizens within its jurisdiction and to secure their well-being. Because persons have dignity and natural rights, they are not mere instrumentalities of the state, i.e., you do not subordinate the individual to the ends of the state. Again, each person possesses a profound inherent and equal dignity, by virtue of his nature, as a rational creature, a creature possessing the God-like powers of reason and freedom. For Christians of Lincoln's era, the truth of this natural law has its origins in biblical teachings that man is made in the image and likeness of God and is entitled to sanctity by all human beings and by the government! Thomas Jefferson's utterances still apply: "We hold these truths to be self-evident, that all men are created equal, that they are endowed by their Creator by certain inalienable rights, that among these are life, liberty and the pursuit of happiness"

Senator William Seward of New York described a "higher law" than the Constitution and said that this law, the natural law of human liberty, dictated the demise of slavery. Question is, in the pursuit of this higher law, did he not (1) deny that the white citizens of the South also were in possession of this right and (2) commit the unpardonable sin of killing the Southern "jailers" to free the slaves? As a professed "Christian," did he not break that commandment "Thou shalt not kill?"

ALL MEN ARE CREATED EQUAL

In both the Declaration of Independence and the Constitution, the Founding Fathers used high-sounding and utopian philosophical utterances to justify their severe rupture with the mother country Britain. Enunciated primarily by Thomas Jefferson, the Declaration described their grievances and failure of an acceptable resolution, concluding that separation and independence was the only satisfactory conclusion to the impasse and tyrannical rule of George III. The *doctrine* that all men, in spite of their differences of character and intelligence, are of equal dignity and worth, and, therefore, entitled to equal rights and privileges in society—equal access to opportunity and equal satisfaction of basic needs—became articulated by Jefferson in his phrase "all men are created equal." This hot-potato phrase became the shibboleth used by the abolitionists to incessantly beat the nation over the head and lobby for the backward primitives from Africa now deprived of these rights as lowly slaves, and how it failed to live up to these lofty principles.

For historical perspective it must be remembered and reemphasized that slavery has had a long history in America (from 1610) and that the institution of slavery was legal in all thirteen colonies when the American Revolution began. It was only when Lincoln achieved the presidency that the issue reached a boiling point in a most horrendous effusion of blood in the American Civil War where the "treatment" with over 1,000,000 troops slain was worse than the "disease" of slavery.

With that same democratic spirit that founded America, the abolitionists and their supporters took up the banner of compassion, and with their utopian vision and broad humanitarianism, combined with evangelistic fervor and holier-than-thou demeanor, they attacked the slave-holders and traders with an in-your-face attitude. They claimed slavery to be an abomination and a sin in the eyes of God without scriptural support! All biblical passages, considered the inspired word of God, declared slavery to be a fact of life to be tolerated and accommodated and not the social injustice that later generations claimed it to be!

Economic and political considerations in favor of supporting and extending slavery into new territories were very powerful elements in the minds of "business-minded" peoples. From a purely economic viewpoint, slave labor was cheaper than free labor (no matter how hard these laborers were squeezed by their employers) and, therefore, slave owners had an economic advantage over their non-slave-owning competitors!

However, the emotional impact of moral considerations, when entered into the equation, effectively trumped all political and economic considerations. Material interests had virtually no standing when confronted with moral issues. It was, therefore, impossible for the South to effectively argue in favor of a system that exploited backward primitives, callously disregarding their feelings when breaking up family units in pursuit of the almighty dollar, the ultimate god worshipped by the materialists. When thusly viewed by the "compassionates," it could justly be called "America's most shameful legacy." By in today's standards, they had the misfortune to be "politically incorrect."

When Thomas Jefferson uttered for all the world to see: "We declare these truths to be self-evident" he did not bother with the difficult task of logical construction and formulation, merely a conclusion. And the world accepted this noble sentiment without question and we have been stuck with it ever since as Gospel truth! Embracing this statement with an all-consuming passion Abraham Lincoln rode this gallant steed like a Don Quixote to right the wrongs of the world, starting with the immediate emancipation of the Negro slave! He would spur his war machine to ever greater and greater feats of brutality and carnage, hurling both friend and foe over the precipice into the valley of death where the river ran wildly with over three million liters of blood!

James Fenimore Cooper, when he wrote "On American Equality" in the American Democrat in 1835, disabuses us of the notion of equality: "The celebrated proposition contained in the Declaration of Independence is not to be understood literally. All men are not created 'equal.'"

"EQUAL"

On his way to his inauguration, Lincoln, in Philadelphia, revealed his obsession with the Declaration's principle of "equality" by crowing, "If this country cannot be saved without giving up that principle—I was about to say—I would rather be assassinated on this spot than to surrender it." To my cynical way of thinking, it is most unfortunate that he was not accommodated in his noble quest. Had he been sent to his final reward, the nation would have been spared the agonies and tremendous loss of life resulting from the Civil War. As is generally known, but cleverly glossed over as a minor footnote, Abraham Lincoln's obsession to immediately bestow the blessings of liberty and equality upon the slaves propelled him to inflict upon the nation the greatest effusion of blood ever to have occurred upon American soil. The deaths of over 1,000,000 brave American souls seem not to have produced commensurate consternation as one would normally opine. Despite the long history of this odious institution—slavery—inuring all to its presence, once he achieved ascendancy to the most powerful seat in the nation, and perhaps the world, it became his immediate goal to free the slaves. He would not delay, he would not compromise, he would not equivocate, he would not consider a "grandfather clause," he would not consider a gradual and compensated emancipation. He rather preferred the dictator's route of immediate butchery of all proslavery supporters and instant emancipation!

In contradistinction to his many years of polishing his craft as an accomplished lawyer, he here eschewed the vigorous exercise of framing his argument by careful step-by-step progressions convincing everyone of the superiority of his logic. Ironically, the framers of the Declaration provided Lincoln with the club by which he beat to death the slaveholders and their supporters "all men are created equal."

From that noble-sounding phrase "all men are created equal," a state of mind is created that insists that because we are created equal in one respect (before the law) then we come to assume equality in all respects, i.e., because men are equally free we claim to be absolutely equal. From this seemingly innocuous utterance, there developed a germ of an idea that took hold of fanatical minds culminating in an avalanche of activity known as the American Civil War where murderous butchery displaced and supplanted ideas and invective. And all because a quasi-despotic leader, Abraham Lincoln, could not countenance negotiation and compromise!

FOUNDATION

From the famous "philosophers" such as Bacon, Descartes, Bayle, Spinoza, Montesquieu, Voltaire, and Rousseau came such illustrious followers as Franklin, Jefferson, Adams, and Madison, and it was these latter illuminaries who brought about an earth-shattering shift in the world's political thought processes. They articulated a basic philosophy of political liberty, intellectual freedom, and equality that together brought about a new, well-ordered form of government. Lincoln, as a politician and a lawyer and lacking exposure to these profound philosophical ideas, even to those ideas in the Declaration of Independence, was determined to uphold the legal principles that Union was an inviolable contract and he would see to it that the South would adhere to this contract even if he had to kill every Southerner to do so!

DECLARATION

Secession went beyond the mundane legal concepts of state's rights, of interposition, of nullification to the lofty philosophical concepts espoused in the Declaration of Independence. These profundities originated from Locke's "Two Treatises of Government" (1689) in which he articulated concepts of natural laws regarding human rights, of individual liberty, of freedom of conscience, and of self-determination. These identical utterances, so nobly articulated in the Declaration of Independence, when repeated by the Confederated States of America, were trashed by the Lincoln administration with tragic consequences to the nation!

The prevailing, dominant philosophical principle upon which the Declaration is founded, and upon which all subsequent actions followed, is the idea of freedom of the individual to establish and secure individual "rights" even if these meant the upsetting the status quo, and turning upside down, the existing and prevailing government. In a subsequent utterance Thomas Jefferson echoed this concept: "Whenever any form of government becomes destructive it is the right of the people to alter or to abolish it and to establish a new government." Thus, it becomes perfectly clear and logical that the South had a perfect "right" to *secede* from the Union when they articulated their own Declaration of Independence (Phase II).

Among all the fanatical, hysterical, and bloodthirsty Northerners, only Horace Greely, who saw the horrendous carnage as a catastrophic event, recommended the South to "go in peace" for had his advice been followed, the carnage that is euphemistically called the American Civil War, would have been averted.

JEAN JACQUES ROUSSEAU 1694–1778

In an original state of nature, people were happy not because they were angels but because they lived entirely for themselves and possessed an absolute independence. In this state of nature people are motivated by a "natural sentiment which inclines every animal to watch over his own preservation, and which directed in man by reason and pity, produces humanity and virtue." But it was the steady growth in numbers of people that forced people together into an arrangement called "society." The problem, says Rousseau, is "to find a form of association which will defend and protect with the whole common force the person and goods of each associate, and in which each, while uniting himself with all, may still obey himself alone."

This "social contract" is the fundamental principle underlying a political association; this principle helps to overcome the lawlessness of absolute license and assures liberty because people willingly adjust their conduct to harmonize with the legitimate freedom of others. What they lose by the social contract is their "natural liberty" and their unlimited right to everything, and what they gain is "civil liberty" and a property right in what they possess.

Unfortunately, unlike Locke, Rousseau concludes that once man has agreed to be a part of "society," there is no turning back, no recourse to tyranny and injustice. He must accept the will of the majority. "This means that he will be forced to be free" to achieve the common good. This assumes the folly that man is always virtuous and will only create "just" laws in this modern world.

Locke, on the other hand, maintained the inviolability of his natural rights that, when government acted unjustly, that man had the right to withdraw from *that* society and form one (with others of like philosophy) that suits them better. Rousseau on the other hand, felt that, for those who could not or would not conform to the general will of society, the government had the right to banish them from that association.

However in his Letter on Virtue, The Individual and Society, written in the spring of 1757, Rousseau admits that it is always possible for a person to turn his back on society and choose voluntary exile, but is of the opinion that the state should take a severe attitude toward the dissatisfied citizen. He elucidates his theory thusly:

> Because my life, my security, my liberty, and my happiness today depend on the cooperation of others like myself, it is clear that I must look upon myself no longer as an isolated individual but as part of a larger whole, as a member of a larger body on whose preservation mine depends absolutely, and any disorder in which I would necessarily feel.
>
> I depend on my native land [*patrie*], at least for my needs, my native land in turn depends for its needs on some other country, and everything is to one degree or another subject to this universal dependency. Natural identity, common weakness, mutual needs, and the society they have made necessary, thus, give me duties and rights common to all men.
>
> You should have quit this life if it was a burden to you and should have quit this country if its laws seemed to you too harsh; die or leave if you wish henceforth to owe me nothing, but pay me for the thirty years of life you have already enjoyed with my assistance. Until you are no longer, you owe me for what you have been.

Thus, it is apparent that unlike Locke, Rousseau's position is that man, while a member of society, has "run up a tab," which he owes to society, and if he wishes to leave that society, he must "pay up" and settle these obligations that he owes to that society.

JOHN LOCKE 1632–1704

In his treatise "Of Civil Government," John Locke holds that in a state of nature each individual may order or control his own life as he alone sees fit free from any restrictions that other men might impose; in this sense he and all others are equal in potentiality and actuality. He has a natural right to be secure in his own person as life is a gift, which no one else has or can claim, as well as the freedom to move about without restriction. As far as "property" is commonly defined, we include the proper possessions, which are gained in working the earth and those that God has given man to use to his advantage and for his convenience. (Classical labor theory of value.)

As was proclaimed in the Declaration of Independence, man had natural rights granted to him by his creator. Locke defined these rights to be life, liberty, and property, but Jefferson, an early pioneer in political correctness, preferred the euphemism life, liberty, and the pursuit of happiness, this last phrase having an infinite number of interpretations (property usually regarded as legal possessions).

Since there is no final authority on earth to whom man can turn for restoration of wrongs committed, it is imperative for man to form a union of common interests in a functioning social unit where a series of laws can be legislated with disinterested judges appointed to adjudicate these conflicts in a peaceful, amicable, and acceptable fashion. Thus, man must surrender his "natural" rights and transfer these rights under *one* body politics, a government functioning to preserve each and every citizens' rights within that framework guided and ruled by a majority of citizen voters.

Of the four requirements Locke believed must be maintained to ensure that it functions for the public good, I refer to only the two which I feel are applicable to the transgressions of Abraham Lincoln in precipitating the most tragic of American history, the Civil War! First, Locke felt that the legislative, i.e., the supreme governmental power, must not use its power arbitrarily over the lives and fortunes of the people. Second, this supreme power cannot take from a man his property without his consent. In both instances Lincoln betrayed the people.

But ultimately, "the community, even after it has delegated its power, does not give up its right of self-preservation, and in this sense retains forever the ultimate power of sovereignty."

"Thus Locke rather cleverly concludes his treatise, not with justification of the right of rebellion, but rather, with the right of the people to put down unlawful government, unlawful that it violates the trust and the law of nature, leading to tyranny, rebellion and dissolution."

THOMAS PAINE

Because of Abraham Lincoln's radical solution (war) in solving the thorny issue of slavery, I sometimes wonder if he understood the fundamental rights of man as articulated in the Declaration of Independence and which originated in the minds of such luminaries as John Locke and Thomas Paine. For instance, Paine's major premise is that individuals were *not* born to their position in life, but *came into the world with basic indestructible rights*. This gave them freedom to make choices about everything, including the type of government they wanted for themselves. He added, "no previous generation had any right to predetermine the nature of this government or to commit subsequent generations to its will." (This coincides with John Locke's assertion that when government becomes destructive of these rights, it is the right of the ruled to abolish or withdraw from this government and create one that is satisfactory to themselves.) Paine wrote: "Man has no property in man, neither has one generation a property in the generations that are to follow." Therefore, I wonder if Lincoln had any familiarity with the concepts of Locke's or Paine's writings, and perhaps even in the Declaration of Independence where it says, "When in the Course of human Events, it becomes necessary for one People to dissolve the Political Bands which have connected them with another."

THOMAS PAINE AND THE DECLARATION OF INDEPENDENCE PHASE II

It is most unfortunate that, in seeking independence, the South did not have a firebrand spokesman as articulate as Thomas Paine to argue on their behalf and to present a unifying vision to counter the clever propaganda constructed by the North. In his article "Common Sense," he excoriates the British as he justifies the independence movement of the colonies from the mother country, Great Britain. Using Paine's words, and wherever Britain is referred to, I have instead inserted "the North" in its place, thereby showing the validity of the Declaration of Independence Phase II as having equal validity to that of Phase I. "I have heard it asserted by some, that as America has flourished under her former connection with Great Britain (the North), the same connection is necessary toward her (the South) future happiness, and will always have the same effect. Nothing can be more fallacious than this kind of argument." "But Britain is the parent country, some say," I would replace Britain with the North. What follows is, "Then the more shame upon her conduct. Even brutes do not devour their young, nor savages make war upon their families; wherefore, the assertion, if true, turns to her reproach." He goes on to say, "This new world hath been the asylum for the persecuted lovers of civil and religious liberty from every part of Europe. Hither have they fled, not from the tender embraces of the mother, but from the cruelty of the monster." Later he says Britain (the North), being now an open enemy, extinguishes every other name and title (neighbor, townsman, countryman, Englishman) and to say that reconciliation is our duty is truly farcical. "Later he goes on, "I challenge the warmest advocate for reconciliation to show a single advantage that this continent can reap, by being connected with Great Britain (the North), I repeat the challenge, not a single advantage is derived."

Further, "But the injuries and disadvantages which we sustain by that connection are without number; and our duty to mankind at large, as well as to ourselves, instruct us to renounce the alliance." Everything that is right or reasonable pleads for separation. The blood of the slain, the weeping voice of nature cries *"tis time to part."*

Although Thomas Jefferson is given credit as being the author of the Declaration of Independence, a document articulating American ideals, true recognition as to the ultimate origin of these profound philosophical concepts must go to the original author, John Locke. The main feature of this document and embraced by the Founding Fathers comes firstly from the recognition of man's natural rights to be free, and upon entering society, has the right to be ruled only by his own consent, and that must be given voluntarily. Further, whenever the rulers are unjust, he has the right to withdraw that consent, revolt if necessary, and remove himself from that unpleasant situation.

Just as the original thirteen colonies claimed a right to revolt against the arbitrary and unjust rule by Britain; so too did the Southern states claim an equal right to revolt against the unjust rule imposed upon them by the North.

THOMAS PAINE: THE RIGHTS OF MAN 1791

In response to Edmund Burke's (the great British statesman) writing "Reflections on the Revolution in France" in which he condemned the many outrages committed during the overthrow of the monarchy of France, Thomas Paine felt obliged to defend the actions of the French in his monumental work "The Rights of Man." He traces the origin of man's inherent rights "to the creation of man" and that he has only lost these rights "because there have been upstart governments, thrusting themselves between, and presumptuously working to unmake man."The illuminating and divine principle of the equal rights of man (for it has its origin from the Maker of man), relates not only to the living individuals, but to generations of men succeeding each other. Every generation is equal in rights to the generations which preceded it, by the same rule that every individual is born equal in rights with his contemporary." He goes on to elucidate, "I mean that all men are all of one *degree,* and consequent that all men are born equal, and with equal natural rights, in the same manner as if posterity had been continued by creation instead of generation… and consequently, every child born into the world must be considered as deriving its existence from God."

He goes on to elucidate man's rights (natural) "are those which appertain to man in right of his existence," i.e., "all the intellectual rights, or rights of the mind and also those rights of acting as an individual for his own comfort and happiness, which are not injurious to the natural rights of others." He goes on: "Civil rights are those which appertain to man in right of his being a member of society" and in that capacity "have those rights better secured." Thus, he distinguishes "that class of natural rights which man retains after entering into society, and those which he throws into the common stock as a member of society."

He summarizes his views into three conclusions: "First, that every civil right grows out of a natural right; or, in other words, is a natural right exchanged.

"Secondly, that civil power, properly considered as such, is made up of the aggregate of that class of natural rights of man, which becomes defective in the individual inpoint of power, and answers not his purpose, but when collected to a focus, becomes competent to the purpose of every one.

"Thirdly, that the power produced from the aggregate of natural rights, imperfect inpower in the individual, cannot be applied to invade the natural rights which are retained in the individual, and in which the power to execute is as perfect as the right itself."

Finally, and most importantly, Paine goes on to discuss the origins of governments and he breaks it down into three sources. "First, superstition. Secondly, power. Thirdly, the common interests of society, and the common rights of man." In the first he describes a theocracy in which all laws came down to man from a superior being handed down to man through intermediaries. In the second he describes a government that was based upon power, and he uses William the Conqueror whose sword assumed the name of Scepter. These people achieved governmental power by conquest and maintained it through military control. To also buttress their claims, they introduced the concept of *divine right* by which they claimed that God blessed and supported their rule! In the third source from which governments have arisen, he describes what has happened here in America as a result of the Revolution. Through the ultimate exercise of man's self-determination, the citizens of the United States banded together to throw off the English government, a form of governance originated from conquest and not society and subsequently rose over the people. Here it was replaced by a *government of the people, by the people and for the people*, the ultimate form of self-determination.

As Paine said it, "The fact therefore must be that the individuals themselves, each in his own personal and sovereign right, entered into a compact with each other to produce a government: and this is the only mode in which governments have a right to arise, and the only principle on which they have a right to exist."

Thus, Lincoln rejects Paine's claims to man's possession of "natural rights" and the preeminence of these talents over society's claim over him. Paine is the philosopher in describing these metaphysical issues; Lincoln, ever the consummate politician, becomes a throwback to those such as William the Conqueror and government by conquest. As an extension of his inherent brutality, he relies on the superior Northern military forces to crush and subdue the South to his will.

Achieving independence from Mother England was one thing; forming a viable and effective form of governance was another. Basically, they struggled with a variety of basic political questions and these had to be determined and clarified. In this new republic, where is the locus of power does it reside with the people, the states or the national government? What are the aims of government: self-preservation, liberty, justice, the promotion of happiness, or the protection of government? In this New World, new approaches to governance could be tried relying on history for guidance but not necessarily ruled by it. It is Hamilton who reveals the strong influence of Locke writings in his conclusion to Federalist No. 22, "The fabric of American empire ought to rest on the solid basis of *the consent of the people*. The streams of national power ought to flow immediately from that pure, original foundation of all legitimate authority."

Because of the confusion in the minds of the Founding Fathers, the United States, from day one, has suffered from an identity crisis that has never been satisfactorily addressed nor resolved. These are: are we "a Union by a Confederacy of sovereign states" or are we "a national government which regards the Union as a consolidation of the States" (Federalist No. 39). The original thirteen colonies were regarded as thirteen separate entities but all British possessions. On breaking free from the mother country, it is logical to assume their continued distinctions when they came to ratify the Constitution as articulated in Federalist No. 39.

On examining the first relation, it appears, on one hand, that the Constitution is to be founded on the assent and ratification of the people of America, given by deputies elected for the special purpose; but, on the other, that this assent and *ratification is to be given by the people, not as individuals composing one entire nation, but as composing the distinct and independent States to which they respectively belong*. It is to be the assent and ratification of the several States, derived from the supreme authority in each state—the authority of the people themselves. The act, therefore, establishing the Constitution will not be a *national* but a *federal* act.

That it will be a federal and not a national act, as these *people regarded in this transaction as forming one nation, the will of the majority of the whole people of the United States would bind the minority in the same manner as the majority in each State must bind the minority* and the will of the majority must be determined either by a comparison of the individual votes, or by considering the will of the majority of the States as evidence of the will of a majority of the people of the United States. Neither of these rules has been adopted. *Each State, in ratifying the Constitution, is considered as a sovereign body, independent of all others, and only to be bound by its own voluntary act.* In this relation, then, the new Constitution will, if established, be a *federal* and not a *national* constitution.

Those who understood we were a nation united as a "Confederacy of sovereign states" (states' rights people usually from the South) declared their "right" to secede from the Union because of the long "history of repeated injuries and usurpations" from the domineering and oppressive treatment by the North. Abraham Lincoln, on the other hand, took the position that we are an inviolable "consolidation of the States" that all the states had signed a legally binding contract, and that he, as a president and an attorney (not as an independent and dispassionate judge) would compel, by force if necessary, the South to abide by the terms of that contract! Even if he had to kill every Southerner and sacrifice many of his own people in the process.

PHILOSOPHICAL PRINCIPLES

The essence of the Declaration of Independence and the Constitution is the philosophical primacy of the individual, his wisdom, and his decency, and the total rejection of all infringements on individual rights. Freedom is the inalienable and universal right of all human beings. Self-government is a manifestation of the universality of these democratic principles!

Even Karl Marx recognized this principle when he said, "The right of man to property is the right to enjoy his possessions and to dispose of the same arbitrarily, without regard to other men, independently from society, the right of selfishness. It is the former individual freedom together with its latter application that forms the basis of civil society. It leads man to see other men not the realization but the limitation of his own freedom. Above all it proclaims the right of man to enjoy and dispose at will of his goods, his revenues and fruits of his work and industry."

For thousands of years the profound philosophical theorists pondered the concepts of natural rights with the sense of human freedom of the will and the power of self-determination. From Plato down through Hobbes, Rousseau, and Locke, these ruminations eventually found expression in the American Declaration of Independence, as articulated by one of America's own philosopher, Thomas Jefferson.

From his book *Individuals and Their Rights* by professor of philosophy Tibor Machan, I give you an updated (1989) version of John Locke's doctrine of natural human rights.

> Human beings are rational animals, with the moral responsibility to excel as such. A good society requires standards for guiding human beings in their conduct toward one another, showing where the proper jurisdiction of one begins and another ends. This is because living in human dignity requires, at least for adults, that persons govern *themselves,* guide their *own lives.* This requirement of freedom from the willful invasion of others ('negative freedom') is promulgated

with a framework of basic human rights in relatively large human communities. This means, roughly, that we need ask no one's permission to live, to take action, and to acquire, hold, or use as we see fit the results of our productivity or creativity. These rights are absolute, inalienable, and universal. Within their scope, that is, in our legal systems, no excuse legitimatizes their violation or infringement. No one can lose these rights, although some actions a person might take can lead to placing that person in circumstances in which he or she must exercise them in very restricted ways (for example, in jail). Every human being has these rights, even when they are not respected by others. And finally, having these rights entitles us to resist, with reasonable force if necessary, attempts by others to violate or infringe them.

PRINCIPLE OF SELF-DETERMINATION

For the last 400 years or so, the global organizing principle has been one of consent. According to Locke, nation-states, being equally sovereign and independent actors, can be bound to legal obligations only to the extent that they have consented to do so. But it was Abraham Lincoln during the time leading up to the Civil War who challenged this concept of "government by consent of the governed" as he refused to countenance allowing the united Southerners to declare themselves free and independent of the oppressive policies of the North even though this line of reasoning paralleled that of the colonies in their squabble with the mother country, and as articulated in the Declaration of Independence

Therefore, judging by Lincoln's behavior and utterances, it seems safe to conclude that, had Lincoln lived at the time of the Founding Fathers, he would have undoubtedly supported the legal justification of Britain in suppressing the colonies and their ridiculous Declaration of Independence and perhaps he might have even applauded the extreme butchery that would have been required for the colonies' submission. The profound philosophical utterances underpinning the Declaration would be ignored and dismissed by Lincoln as irrelevant. His would be a narrow focus on the *legality* of the move and he would argue the issue in any court of law for that's what he did for a living—arguing in court and debating on the hustings. And quite successfully, I might add.

AGE OF ENLIGHTENMENT

French philosophers Voltaire (1691–1778), Montesquieu (1689–1755), Diderot (1713–1784), Condorcet (1742–1794), and others, were of the opinion that human reason provides the most reliable guide to man's destiny. Rousseau, considered a romantic in the Age of Reason, believed that the stability of a society is based upon a set of opinions or values, which the majority accepts as the rule for its thought and behavior. In the state of nature, people are content because they live entirely for themselves, were responsible only to themselves and were absolutely independent. They are motivated entirely by self-interest—by love of self (amour de soi) and by impulses, which ensure his own preservation, based upon his natural instincts, cunning and reason—a Social Darwinian concept before the age of Darwin (survival of the fittest).

With the steady growth in numbers, people are brought together to form a society: "a form of association which will defend and protect, with the whole common force, the person and goods of each associate, and in which each, while uniting himself with all, may still obey himself alone." This "social contract" requires each individual to adjust his conduct to harmonize with the legitimate freedom of others. The common good becomes the ideal.

But what is a member to do if his own impulses are incompatible with the whole? It was John Locke (1632–1704) who already articulated a philosophical answer to this apparent dilemma. It is by *his own consent* that man makes himself a member of some politic society, and it is also by *his own consent* that he may withdraw his support of that society and then join one that is more agreeable to his liking. Locke would never agree that the transferal of his rights to the sovereign was irrevocable.

When one reads reference books on the Age of the Enlightenment, or the Age of Reason, we find it described as an intellectual movement of the seventeenth and eighteenth centuries characterized by a celebration of the powers of human reason, a keen interest in science, a promotion of religious tolerance, and a desire to construct governments free of tyranny. The ideal model of reason, that distinguished truth from superstition, was that of John Locke declaring that what was reasonable was also natural and universal, and must be accorded primacy in fashioning a modus vivendi or method of living.

In my mind, a question arises. Did the Age of Enlightenment die in America once the American Revolution came to a successful outcome? Once freedom had been achieved and a democratic form of government established, did the nation withdraw into a shell and regress into the Dark Ages where ignorance flourished and classical culture was stifled, all because the barbarians took over? During the Enlightenment tolerance and rationality overcame ignorance and barbarity. However, during the American Civil War, it became perfectly clear that the reverse characterized that period of time. The barbarian, Abraham Lincoln, perpetrated the moral perversion of classifying slavery as a sin (*whereas* the Bible supports that institution with few caveats) and the killing of over 1,000,000Americans to correct that sin (despite the biblical injunction) as eminently justifiable!

THE AGE OF ENLIGHTENMENT, REASON, RATIONALISM

In the November 29, 2004, issue of the Weekly Standard, Diana Schaub, who teaches political science at Loyola College in Maryland, observed the long-lasting and pervasive effects of the Enlightenment upon American philosophical thinking and behavior. She tells us: "America's Enlightenment tradition, however, is flourishing. The institutions established by the Founding Fathers still shape the American character; the documents they penned are the objects of our political reasoning and our partisan debates; and their personal example is still found worthy of study and often of emulation (as attested by the spate of bestselling biographies read by ordinary citizens)."

If this is the case, where reason is deemed supreme in all the departments of intellectual inquiry, where Locke's enunciation of the primacy of individual's rights, "there remains in the people a supreme power to remove or alter the legislative where they find the legislative act contrary to the trust reposed in them," then we must conclude that Abraham Lincoln ignored this principle that was carved in stone in the Declaration of Independence.

FUNDAMENTAL RIGHTS

The American Revolution (and the French Revolution) meant that the principles of liberty and equality on which modern liberal democracy is based had finally been discovered and implemented. Unfortunately, since that time, we have not progressed in any fundamental sense. Indeed it can be argued that the crushing of the South in the American Civil War has retarded the historical process and set back peoples' struggle for self-realization at least 150 years. Liberal democracies, as political systems based on popular sovereignty with guarantees of individual rights, have only now recovered from the crushing blow inflicted by Abraham Lincoln in America! Any thoughts paralleling those of the American and French revolutions were subdued and virtually nonexistent.

The actions of Lincoln invalidated the very spirit of the Declaration of Independence and the Constitution. The inalienable rights we once cherished were a priori rights and conditions of existence given to us not by man but given to us by God. As such these a priori rights cannot legitimately be taken away from human life forms, i.e., once created, humans have rights guaranteed by God.

It was the absolutist, polarized positions on both sides that hindered rational discussions of the issues, issues so emotionally colorized that rendered dispassionate discussions impossible. Here I find it appropriate to insert Immanuel Kant's categorical imperative: "Every man is to be respected as an absolute end in himself; and it is a crime against the dignity that belongs to him as a human being, to use him as a mere means for some external purpose."

SOCIAL CONTRACT

J. J. Rousseau's "Social Contract" refers to a concept upon which other philosophers, e.g., Hobbes and Locke, also have believed that the state was the outcome of a covenant or agreement among men to be ruled by that state, and further the purpose of the state was the protection of those people to which it owes its being. But a prerequisite for this arrangement is that the state must have enough power to provide such protection and, therefore, some believed that the sovereignty must be unified and absolute. According to Hobbes, men must choose to be ruled or to be free; liberty went out with anarchy and security went with civil obedience. To be secure man must submit to the power of the sovereign, it is by making this social compact and living under law that man achieves security and peace.

But Locke insists that man is free if he retains sovereignty over himself and if he enacts the rules or laws and which he is obliged to obey. He maintains that if the government breaches the trust that we put in them "they forfeit the power of the people had put in their hands… and it devolves to the people, who have a right to resume their original liberty and by the establishment of the new legislative (such as they shall think fit) provide for their own safety and security."

NATURAL RIGHTS—ELIZABETH CADY STANTON (1815–1902)

Although Elisabeth Cady Stanton is not considered as a philosopher, instead a feminist and an abolitionist, some of her utterances and observations are reminiscent of such notables as John Locke. In her book *Solitude of Self*, she expands on the concept of natural and individual rights and waxes eloquently on the majesty of "self." She tells us that every human life contains a precious inner world or space that is rightly called the "conscience" and "our self." Included in "conscience" is the power of autonomous choice, a deeply precious commodity. This "right of individual conscience and judgment" and "birthright to self-sovereignty" gives everyone the freedom of choice and self-development. It is our right because of the depth and preciousness of the self. "Rich and poor, intelligent and ignorant, wise and foolish, virtuous and vicious man and woman; it is ever the same, each soul must depend only on itself!"

PRINCIPLE OF SELF-GOVERNMENT

Historians tell us that when the Missouri Compromise was repealed by Stephen A. Douglas, Senator from Illinois, Abraham Lincoln became disturbed, but when the Kansas-Nebraska Act as passed in 1864, opening Federal territories that were not yet states to slavery, he became aroused as never before and became galvanized into reentering politics to work for its repeal. At the state fair in Springfield, on October 4,1854, he replied to a speech given by Douglas the day before. In it he said he hated the spread of slavery "because of the monstrous injustice of slavery itself."

Arguing further he goes on. "The doctrine of self-government is right, absolutely and eternally right. Then to argue against slavery: When the white man governs himself, that is self-government, but when he governs himself, and *another* man, that is *more* than self-government—that is despotism." Further he says, "What I do say is, that no man is good enough to govern another man without that other's consent. I say this is the leading principle—the sheet anchor of American republicanism. Our declaration of Independence says, "We hold these truths to be self-evident" that all men are created equal; that they are endowed by their Creator with certain inalienable rights; that among these are life, liberty, and the pursuit of happiness. That to secure these rights, governments are instituted among men, deriving their just powers from the consent of the governed."

This last phrase, "from the consent of the governed" is the critical one he hangs himself on his own petard. In his eagerness to bestow the rights of democratic participation upon the black slaves he is willing to deprive the whites of that same democratic principle! In *their* declaration of independence, they have preferred to withdraw their support and consent to be governed by that government in Washington, deciding instead to put their trust and consent to be governed by another government (in Richmond)

RIGHTS

Much has been written of Lincoln's seeming obsession with the phrase "government of the people, by the people and for the people" yet no one seems to notice the nuance that, as he preoccupied with providing these concepts, he, at the same time, trashed the philosophical concepts regarding the "rights of the people." Government of the people, by the people, and for the people was that form of government which Lincoln defined and provided for them. No contrary opinion was allowed and no appeals were to be made. The South, along with the North, had signed a legal document uniting the thirteen colonies into a Federal association, and it was Lincoln's opinion that this *legal* document was binding upon all members in perpetuity and, according to him, they had no right to withdraw, secede, leave, abrogate, or opt out of this eternal Union. With the powers invested in him as president, he would be judge, jury, and chief enforcement officer to force compliance with this legal document even if he had to kill every one South of the Mason-Dixon line!

PRINCIPLES OF CONSENT

If we consider the political units called nation-states and their structural characteristics we find that the South possessed all the features that virtually guarantee its existence and perpetuation as a cohesive unit or nation. It (the population) is in possession of a well-defined territory, a common language, religious outlook, race (Anglo-Saxon), its own economic patterns, a common history and tradition, a common set of customs and principles all leading to a particular collective identity and destiny. Although the "nation" (sovereign state) remains the final arbiter over the lives of its citizens, John Locke argues that the freedom of man and liberty of acting according to his own will, being grounded on reason, permits man to opt out of any situation of arbitrary power, i.e., to withdraw his consent to be ruled by *that* government and place his consent with a government more in keeping with his own philosophical outlook. He, by natural law, has the power to incorporate himself with any commonwealth or to agree with others to begin a new one.

Perhaps George Will articulated a crass version of this same philosophy when he asked and said, "Are human beings only mildly social creatures, moved primarily by the desire for self-preservation and avoidance of the 'inconveniences' that the state of nature has for property holders? Do they, therefore, enter into only chilly political associations with other materialistic individuals who are similarly motivated by private interests?" No matter how the ideas are conveyed, the same basic principle applies. Whereas, in a pure state of nature man has to rely entirely upon himself for all aspects of his existence, and whereas, in a social state he must forego the idea of total self-reliance, and blend with others of like mind to combine their reciprocal energies for the good of all. But this does *not* mean he must surrender his freedom of choice to leave that group and join with another group more compatible with his new outlook and philosophy. He still maintains his God-given freedoms!

SELF-DETERMINATION

Concepts of human rights have been a major feature of American thought right from the day of its birth in 1776. Thomas Jefferson, as one of the major enunciators of the Declaration of Independence, articulated "self-evident" truths that all men are created equal, that they are endowed by their creator with certain unalienable rights that among these are "life, liberty, and the pursuit of happiness." Echoing John Locke's pronouncements of one hundred years previously that, if government fails society in its liberties, "it devolves to the people, who have a right to resume their original liberty, and by the establishment of a new legislative (such as they shall think fit) provide for their own safety and security, which is the end for which they are in society." Jefferson similarly asserts "it is their right, it is their duty, to throw off such a government and provide for their future security."

Therefore to me it seems ironic, if not hypocritical, for Abraham Lincoln, in his Gettysburg Address to dare utter the words, "We here highly resolve that these dead shall not have died in vain—that this nation, under God, shall have a new birth of freedom—and that government of the people, by the people, for the people, shall not perish from the earth." For it was *he* who violently stood in the way of the South's attempt at freedom from the tyranny of Washington, to determine its own course of government of *their* people, by *their* people, for *their* people by slaughtering them by the thousands.

In the British parliament, debates raged long and often as to the advisability of recognizing the Confederacy. Many Tories, Whigs, and Liberals had supported the moves for self-determination by the Greeks, Italians, Hungarians, and others, saw an element of hypocrisy, when the Northern "children of revolution" took up arms to prevent their Southern brethren from proclaiming their independence from an equally oppressive (as the British) North. Workers in Lancashire cotton mill towns and Liverpool Dockers accepted unemployment and starvation secondary to the cotton famine that resulted from Lincoln's blockade of the Southern U.S. ports. Moral considerations regarding slavery trumped the slaughter of their "brothers" in the South.

NATURAL RIGHTS

Whether we attribute it to capitalism or democracy, both ideas possess the concept of ultimate freedom for self-realization; they are both based upon the concept of freedom of individuals to pursue their own self-interest, capitalism in the economic sphere, democracy in the political and social sphere. Individual rights, the right of each individual to his own life and to the pursuit of his own happiness, neither sacrificing himself to others nor others to himself is the Lockean philosophical basis upon which this country is founded. Everyone should be allowed to better his situation in life. The brutal suppression of the South's desire to break away from the North and form an association of like-minded people in a union of the Confederate States of America, even to the extent of butchering (and being butchered) of over 1,000,000 Americans was considered "excusable" and even "rational" by Abraham Lincoln and his supporters.

Conveniently, they ignored the doctrine of inalienable natural rights found in the Declaration of Independence (derived from John Locke). Chapter 5 of Locke's treatise shows how allowing people the freedom to advance their own economic and political situation through hard labor and industry inevitably increases the material and political well-being of all. Locke demonstrated how a liberal, constitutional order offers the greatest opportunity for human beings of superior political ambition and those of superior entrepreneurial talent to benefit all mankind. Lincoln had other ideas as he trashed and traduced this philosophical profundity.

Over the years, and especially most recently, American society has evolved greatly with regards to individual rights so that there is a plethora of them: we have civil rights, privacy rights, gay rights, feminism, reproductive choice, sexual freedom, and the right to worship as we please and the right not to worship at all! It is through the activity of various elements of our society that has clamored for special consideration for "basic human rights," which are educed from the Constitution and the Bill of Rights. True democracy allows its citizens maximum freedom for progress and evolution in many spheres including those of "rights."

SPIRIT OF INDEPENDENCE

In the Letters to the Editor of the Wall Street Journal, December 18, 2006, there appeared one from Alex Salmond, a member of the British Parliament and Leader of the Scottish National Party. In it he tells us that in 1707, the Treaty of Union united Scotland and England to form Great Britain. At the time it was considered unpopular by the general populace but a pragmatic economic one by their leaders. Now, in this twenty-first century, Scotland is planning to become "an equal member in the community of nations," i.e., declaring their *independence* from England!

We are told this urge for independence has a long history for, according to him, our Declaration of Independence was largely based on their Scottish Declaration of Arbroath. This mentality was exported to America and he tells us more than half of the signatories to the Declaration of Independence were Scots; they provided the "intellectual backbone of the American independence movement."

I think it extremely unlikely that London would follow the coarse example of Abraham Lincoln to force the Scots back into the Union. That type of tyrannical, dictatorial mentality of a brute is no longer an appropriate mechanism in this twenty-first century. More than likely, patient, protracted, and laborious negotiation and compromise would be the order of the day.

Evolution of the ideas of democracy and individual rights came from the recognition that all global citizens are equal and as such deserving of the indisputable rights enjoyed by those who first benefited from it.

"God grants liberty to those who respect, love and defend it."

DEMOCRACY

In the general historical accounts of the United States of America, it is conceded that the philosophical foundations of our system of government (democratic) are derived from that of the ancient Greeks. Yet when we read of Jean Jacques Rousseau, a philosopher and French political theorist (1712–1778), we find ideas that resonate with our concepts of government of the people, by the people and for the people. As outlined in his "Social Contract" (1762), there is the concept of a just state based on the general consent of the governed. His theory granted unlimited sovereignty and absolute right to oversee the actions of the government, to the general will, that is, to the community of citizens. (people)

Since this was written sometime before the American Revolution, it becomes very easy to speculate the influence of his writings and theories upon the Founding Fathers. After the French Revolution in 1789, when the Declaration of the Rights of Man and the Citizen was written, many historians attribute the ideals therein to the Declaration of Independence and the Constitution whereas they clearly had a prior origination in the mind of Rousseau.

Thus, we can see the historical progression, the percolation of the concept of self-determination down through the ages popping its head up here and there where philosophy transcended brutality in political affairs. It is to Rousseau's ideas of liberté, egalité, and fraternité, and the profound philosophical utterances of John Locke that persuaded the Founding Fathers of the superiority of such a system finding a home in the new world.

PRINCIPLES OF DEMOCRACY

In the October issue of the New Republic, a Mr. Amartya Sen, a Nobel Prize winner in Economics in 1998, presents us with an interesting essay on the origins and principles of that process called democracy. Although there is much to praise in this comprehensive presentation, there are two comments/observations which caught my eye and with which I heartily agree. He says, "To ignore the centrality of public reasoning in the idea of democracy not only distorts and diminishes the history of democratic ideas, it also detracts attention from the interactive processes through which a democracy functions and on which its success depends." Calm rational debates with a process of give and take in compromising polar positions and arriving at a consensus are characteristic features of the democratic process. His second comment, "The alternative—trying to cure the defects of democratic practice through authoritarianism and the suppression of public reasoning—increases the vulnerability of a country to sporadic disasters," is fertile ground for critical assessment of the democratic process during the American Civil War

By abandoning the historic tried and true avenues of negotiation and compromise in dealing with the South's own Declaration of Independence, by not persuading them through reason and debate the folly of their course, he failed as a leader to avert the calamity that horrendously followed. Instead, by resorting immediately to the sword, he showed himself to have bungled as a diplomatic leader, and yet the bullshitters have portrayed his actions as a firm and heroic effort the "preserve and save the Union." But at what cost? The graves of 1,000,000 soldiers, North and South, are a stark irrefutable testament to his abject failure as a supposed "great leader." His "authoritarianism and suppression of public reason" plunged the nation over the edge and into the abyss.

From numerous sources we read that man's capacity to reason is the major feature that separates man from the animal kingdom where reflexive, unthinking actions are the norm. Lincoln, instead of using a higher faculty, succumbed to and descended down into the behavior patterns of the animal kingdom—reflexive animal passions to strike out, attack, kill his fellow man—possessed by an all-consuming blind rage to impose his iron will!

Thus, to portray him as a compassionate, caring thoughtful man is the ultimate hypocrisy and insult to the thinking man's intelligence. Historical characterization as such, is a blatant lie and the ultimate dishonesty perpetrated by charlatans. That he has achieved near sainthood is a tribute to the propaganda success of his admirers and historical portrayers. It is through the eyes of honest observation and reflection, avoiding the rhetoric, propaganda, and bullshit that the inescapable conclusion must be that Abraham Lincoln was an incompetent chief executive blindly pursuing rigid, uncompromising policies that clearly brand him as a butcher!

PROPERTY

In his writings, John Locke states: "The supreme power (government) cannot take from any man any part of his property without his own consent. For the preservation of property being the end of government, and that for which man enters into society." In the Declaration of Independence, the American colonists proclaimed also that man possessed natural rights granted to them by their creator that governments were instituted by man with their consent to protect their rights. To Locke these were life, liberty, and property. In an early draft, Jefferson used these exact same words but for whatever reasoning (political correctness?) changes "property" to "the pursuit of happiness." According to Locke's line of reasoning, I feel certain that he would conclude Abraham Lincoln had no right to abolish slavery nor to declare emancipation and, most importantly, to have declared war upon the South. For hundreds of years prior to Lincoln and the abolitionists, slaves were regarded by everyone, North and South, as property. Disregarding and defying his responsibility as a government executive to protect the rights of his constituents to protect property he highhandedly acted not to do his sworn duty. When Locke talked of "rebellion," he was referring to a denial of civil society and a return to natural state of man before becoming part of a greater social group.

It was in these times that the profound thinkers as Locke changed the philosophical thinking by placing instead human beings at the center of things, human beings seen as individuals with their private interests and frailties and limited rationality and as the products of historical and social change. The science of government became profoundly different after Hume's argument, as former professor of history at Georgetown University put it, that "self-interest is all there is. The overriding guiding force in all our actions is not our reason, or our sense of obligation to others, or any innate moral sense-all these are simply formed out of habit and experience- but the most basic human passion of all, the desire for self-gratification. It is the one thing human beings have in common. It is also the necessary starting point of any system of morality, and of any system of government."

The purpose of government lay exclusively in the furtherance of the happiness of the governed. Its fundamental duty in this respect was to safeguard the liberties that were an inalienable quality of citizenship. Lincoln failed to observe and respect this right!

Lincoln refused to recognize unequivocally the right of the South to its own self-determination, to independent institutions, political, social, cultural, and most importantly, economic, that express the character of their Southern life as they chose to develop it!

Although Senator Joseph Biden is not known as a profound thinker, he was quoted as saying this philosophical utterance (and immediately ignored its implications as he targeted legendary jurist Robert Bork), "As a child of God, I believe my rights are not derived from the Constitution. My rights are not derived from any government. My rights are not derived from any majority. My rights are because I exist. They are given to me and each of my fellow citizens by our Creator and they represent the essence of human dignity."

The concept of "rights" are pillars upon which was articulated the Declaration of Independence. This concept had its origin with the ancient Greeks and had an inexorable flow in the minds of Hobbes, Locke, Rousseau, and eventually to the Founding Fathers only to hit a brick wall in the inflexible mind of Abraham Lincoln! Even had Jefferson Davis uttered Biden's profundities they would have been rejected by Lincoln. It was Lincoln who carried the nation as he trashed the "rights" of the Southerners when they dared to declare their independence from the oppressor North. He in essence said I have the majority behind me and will deny rights to you, the minority, simply because I can, and you do not have the power to stop me. To hell with the highly educated and profound thinking scholars. I, Lincoln, the politician, have the power to crush these people and their highfalutin ideas!

At the time of the Revolution, the idea of natural rights was injected into the debates and was the impetus for demands for independence from the mother country, Britain. This concept of natural rights, which are possessed by all people and which cannot be taken away by any government, were philosophical concepts first articulated by the Greeks and later refined by Hobbes, Locke, and Rousseau. Jefferson incorporated it as a cornerstone of the Declaration of Independence when he wrote: "We hold these truths to be self-evident, that all men are created equal, that they are endowed by their Creator with certain unalienable Rights, that among these are Life, Liberty and the Pursuit of Happiness."

This inconsistency and conflict of natural rights ideology with the presence of the institution of slavery was seized upon by the antislavery advocates to bludgeon the proslavery advocates mercilessly. However, when the South attempted a parallel argument of their "unalienable rights" or the right to find its own future and pursue its own destiny to justify their attempts at secession, Abraham Lincoln refused to recognize this lofty philosophical concept and proceeded to butcher the South to force them to stay in the Union. With the force of his iron will, he kept the Union intact, but at what price? The 1,000,000 dead souls decry this height of hypocrisy but obviously to no avail.

Amongst all the sacred rules, precepts, and commands of the Almighty given for man to observe and keep was the one particularly applicable "Thou shalt not kill." To right the "wrong" that slavery represented they would somehow conveniently ignore or overlook this clear and unequivocally prescription. And these people claim to be Christians!

LIBERTY

Liberty has sometimes been described as an aberration in mankind's history—a light that has flared here and there over the centuries, only to dissolve back into the darkness. Also, the institutions of government are meant to support the liberties of the people as opposed to the ambitions of the state. Judging by those two aphorisms, I am reminded of a clever sentence by Mark Twain: "There are certain sweet-smelling sugar-coated lies current in the world which all politic men have apparently tacitly conspired together to support and perpetuate."

EVOLUTION

A significant document expressing respect for human dignity and human rights was the Helsinki Final Act of 1975, an unsung achievement of President Gerald Ford. It contains the following startling words: "The participating States will respect human rights and fundamental freedoms, including the freedom of thought, conscience, religion or belief, for all without distinction as to race, sex, language or religion. The participating States will respect the equal rights of peoples and their right to self-determination." Again and again and again, the most fundamental ideal of the inalienable rights of the individual resurfaces time after time after time in the course of our history yet no one has had the temerity to point out how outrageously Lincoln traduced this philosophy as he butchered the South!

DECLARATION

UNION

The organization of the original thirteen colonies into a unified entity was purely an effort to create a consolidated force to bring about the likelihood of a successful rupture and independence from the mother country, Britain. This single entity, with a unified outlook with shared experiences and grievances, was paramount in dealing with their common adversary. It was moreover, a union of two disparate societies, two strange bedfellows: the shrewd, opportunistic, capitalistic, and industrial North, and the agrarian, slave-holding, and aristocratic South, who took on airs of the landed gentry, contemptuous of the laboring classes.

It was like a marriage where each party pledged their fidelity to the other. Unhappily, in their zeal to embrace the concepts of liberty and independence from the oppressive and tyrannical rule of Britain, the South threw caution to the wind and blindly accepted the promises by the North and joined forces with them to fight the common enemy. Had they insisted on a prenuptial agreement, where the issue of their property (slaves) was clearly delineated and secured, there would have been no causus belli, there would have been no Civil War! If the North would have refused then the South would have had reason to reject this offer of marriage, (union) and the North would have been left high and dry to face the British assaults… alone! The leaders would surely have been hung, and we might still be under the Crown!

The South certainly had grounds for a divorce from the oppressive, tyrannical behavior of the North (spousal abuse?) Abraham Lincoln would hear none of it. He would bind the South to the North with "hoops of steel" to preserve this Union even if he had to kill every Southerner to force compliance!

Some historians and writers, James B. D. DeBow among them, emphasized the ethnic and cultural differences between the North and the South and insisted that in 1779 a foolish experiment to "erect one nation out of two irreconcilable peoples" had occurred. The Southern whites he claims were descended from the English Cavaliers, and the "Yankees" were descended from the Puritan Roundheads and because of these major differences, when friction occurred, another Declaration of Independence by the South from the North was the only sensible solution.

The Union Secretary of the Navy, Gideon Welles, a "Yankee," blamed the Civil War on the "diseased imagination" of the Southerners "who… fancied themselves cavaliers… They came ultimately to believe themselves a superior and better race, knights of blood and spirit. Only a war could wipe out this arrogance and folly"! This remarkable utterance is but another manifestation of the bloodthirsty attitude of the Lincoln cabinet and that pervaded the whole North.

Believing, much as in the original Declaration of Independence, that they too had the right to secede from the Union, South Carolina issued theirs on December 24,1860. "We, therefore, the People of South Carolina, by our delegates assembled, appealing to the Supreme Judge of the world for the rectitude of our intentions, have solemnly declared that the Union heretofore existing between this State and the other States of North America, is dissolved, and that the State of South Carolina has resumed her position among the other nations of the world, as a separate and independent State, with full power to levy war, conclude peace, contract alliances, establish commerce, and to do all other acts and things which independent States may of a right to do."

Mississippi, Florida, Alabama, Georgia, Louisiana, and Texas soon joined South Carolina. In February 1861, a congress met in Montgomery, Alabama, to adopt a constitution for the new Confederated States of America with Jefferson Davis as its president. It was only after the firing on Fort Samter that Virginia, Arkansas, North Carolina, and Tennessee also joined the Confederacy.

Refusing to recognize and accept the fact that the institution of slavery was an integral part in the fabric of the South's economic and social structure Abraham Lincoln and his Northern accomplices would also refuse to recognize and accept the rational, logical, and sane solution and/or alternative, to separate themselves from the South and its odious practice by letting them go their own way seeking their own destiny (and the North's hands are cleansed) by allowing them to secede from the Union. Instead, propelled by the righteous anger of a compassionate idealist, blinded with rage of a rejected suitor, he would mercilessly murder them for their impertinence, brutalize the citizens, lay waste to the countryside, and the brainless historians dare insist he was our "greatest president"!

A NATION OF STATES

In the initial Constitutional Convention in 1787, the delegates came as representatives of twelve sovereign states (Rhode Island refused to send delegates), states that had developed independently and separately as colonies, entities now banding together in a loose confederation of "states" to obtain their collective liberty from the mother country Britain. A major and persistent consideration in the debates was that of states' rights: would the states be represented as equal entities or by population? What power would be taken away from the states in forming a central government? How could a national supreme government be formed without completely eviscerating the power of the states? Patrick Henry, the great firebrand, completely befuddled by the seemingly insoluble dilemma is said to have uttered, "The question turns, sir, on that poor little thing… the expression, 'We, the people, instead of the States of America.' What right had they to say, '*We* the people? Who authorized them to speak the language of 'We the people'; instead of 'We the states'?"

The concepts of the Declaration of Independence were produced through the courage, imagination, and idealism of the Founding Fathers. Subsequently it led to liberalism, revolution, nationalism, democracy, and finally republicanism. Through this Declaration the Founding Fathers expressed the Enlightenment view that man attains happiness by *freely* developing his capacities and not by submitting them to someone else's arbitrary authority. Men in positions of power, especially over a long period of time, tend to feel omniscient and omnipotent, and then tend to rule arbitrarily, without consideration for other opinions.

From day one America has operated with the belief, mistaken or not, that it had a unique historical mission, some consider divinely inspired, beginning with the image of the city upon a hill and progressing through manifest destiny. Woodrow Wilson seemed to articulate this vision that we are "to show the way to the nations of the world how they shall walk in the paths of liberty. It was of this that we dreamed at our birth." Apparently, Abraham Lincoln too was possessed by this mania as he "show(ed) the way to the (South) how they should walk in the paths of liberty" forever that he would use such murderous brutality in

None gives him credit for recognizing his "peoples" rights to seceded from the Union following the higher principles based on the concepts of human equality, personal liberty, individual rights, participatory government, and the rule of law. They, thus, imply these concepts were above his limited capacity of philosophical discourse and understanding. Perhaps he, better than Lincoln, understood the Declaration of Independence. "When in the course of human events it becomes necessary for one people to dissolve the political bands which have connected them with another…" Later, he would claim that the Civil War had settled only the question of power, not the question of principle!

Memorials
Erected by (city, town, or group)
In honor of
The heroic valor
and patriotic service
of her sons during the
Civil War

TO OUR COUNTRY'S DEFENDERS

The above inscription is a sample of many found on numerous statues, tablets, stained-glass windows, and other monuments erected and dedicated throughout the North to honor the dead and give meaning to the "cause" for which they needlessly died. Go to the many cities and towns in the North, observe and study these, to me, grotesque memorials erected to portray the war as a noble cause for which so many Americans (on both sides) perished. Erected by prominent artists, paid for by prominent citizens, these majestic, ostentatious memorials displayed a false concern for the sacrifices made by the youth of America, possessed of enormous potential their life's blood oozing back to Mother Earth, unused and, therefore, wasted. They are remembrances of the enormous number of lives lost but, in fact, are monuments to man's stupidity, to his dark side in dealing with his fellow American.

The overall presentation of the historical account of the Civil War would lead readers to believe that the North was fighting a fiendish, implacable, and malignant foe intent upon the subjugation of the peace-loving Northerners and, therefore, deserving of death. It was American fighting American, brother fighting brother, the ultimate tragedy and stupidity! It was butchery of gargantuan proportions, never equaled nor exceeded in any conflict in which America was involved. The number of total dead in the Civil War was over 600,000! I cannot overemphasize the brutal fact that this number exceeds the sum total of all the dead of *all* the wars in which the United States was involved! A monstrous travesty!

The memorials are also a continual reminder of the misguided compassion and zeal of the abolitionists in their quest to create a utopia, a Garden of Eden in this New World where "all men are created equal" would be a reality, not merely a profound philosophical utterance.

THE BIBLE AND THE ABOLITION

DEMOCRACY AND SLAVERY

As a basic premise and foundation in their argument against slavery, the abolitionists were quick to point out that slavery was incompatible with the noble concepts of democracy.

It was their unshakeable belief that these two ideas were contradictory and mutually exclusive in a society such as ours. Americans are quick to boast how they acquired these noble philosophical concepts of democracy, of self-rule, from the ancient Greeks but seem to be woefully ignorant of, or conveniently overlook, the glaring fact that America also received from them the seemingly callous or, at least, matter-of-fact attitude in regards to the institution of slavery. There in ancient Greece and for over two hundred years in America, it was "no big deal" to buy, sell, and own slaves and to control them as the owner seemed fit and appropriate. The ancient Greeks viewed this practice in a cool, calculating and dispassionate manner, whereas the politically correct abolitionists and their allies in America seemed intent on persuading the nation that slavery was, moreover, a hideous, evil, and odious habit that all moral people must abolish immediately!

Consistent with this dispassionate view toward slavery the Greeks developed a businesslike method of emancipating or freeing their slaves. Apart from voluntary manumission by their owners, slaves could achieve freedom from other ways. Some could be freed by the payment of ransom by friends and relatives (as in the case of Plato). In some instances, the state could free the slaves for service in war but was required to indemnify the owners. Lastly, the slave himself could buy his own freedom by the money accumulated through the years of his servitude. If a slave is subjected to great cruelty he has an avenue of escape. By fleeing to a temple he forces his master to sell him.

Unfortunately, in America, raging passions, pros, and cons, prevented the appropriate people from achieving such an enlightened, cerebral, and unemotional solution to the problem of slavery. It is said that Plato condemned the enslavement of Greeks by Greeks but accepted slavery for all others on the ground that some people have "underprivileged minds." Aristotle looked upon the slave as an animate tool and would continue to do menial work until such time as the invention of "machines." It might have been a humanitarian sentiment that moved the leaders of the North to insist on freedom for the slaves, but it was the complete lack of negotiating skills by a rigid, unbending, and determined leader, Abraham Lincoln, that resulted in the bloodiest solution imaginable, the American Civil War!

HYPOCRITE

While denying he cared not whether slavery was voted up or down Lincoln cleverly rises above the common debate to insert a more profound philosophical view in discussing his fierce love of liberty: "Our defense is in the 'spirit' which prizes liberty as the heritage of all men, in all lands everywhere. Destroy this spirit and you have planted the seeds of despotism at your own doors."

EARLIEST PROPOSAL FOR THE ABOLITION OF SLAVERY

On February 11, 1790, two delegations (Quaker), one from New York and the other from Philadelphia, presented petitions to the House, calling for the federal government to put an end to the African slave trade despite Article 5, Section 9, Paragraph I of the Constitution which read: "The Migration or Importation of such Persons as any of the states now existing shall think proper to admit, shall not be prohibited by the Congress prior to the Year one thousand eight hundred and eight."

Because Abraham Lincoln felt the South's Declaration of Independence as irrational, illegal, and impermissible, he showed his unconcern with abstract and philosophical principles and by doing so put himself in the camp of (Mad) King George III who declared the original Declaration of Independence as worthless and an insult to the Royal Crown!

Throughout all his speechifying, we see in Abraham Lincoln as a man of profound idealism; a man who would, if he could, right all the wrongs of the world, and when he became president of the United States with its attendant enormous power, and considering slavery to be evil, embarked on a divine mission, a moral crusade, to see that the evildoers were punished. Apparently, he and the nation's historians view the loss of over 1,000,000 loyal Americans as a minor incident in the big picture. He, along with the abolitionists, felt that the buying, selling, trading, and exploiting of slaves was the greater evil; they must be eradicated and the slaves set free!

MORAL RELATIVISM

Abolitionists insist on claiming the moral high ground, that the abolition of slavery was, and still is the ultimate in man's humanitarian accomplishments. The altruistic urge to free the oppressed slave followed by the "noble" battle that brought about their freedoms reflected the mindset of these abolitionists who, inebriated by the concepts of liberty and equality, became intent on bestowing it upon the slaves.

In all the voluminous history of that era no one wants to assign blame or accept responsibility for causing that "terrible war." Was it really God's will, a retribution upon mankind for the offence of slavery? Or was it merely a collection of forces of political machines in smoke-filled rooms, using Lincoln as a tool to further and protect their financial interests? Although quoting much from the Bible, he was not an agent through whom God spoke or acted. He was portrayed by many as a secular saint, an angel of mercy, bestowing freedom upon the slave population. Those in the South might consider him an angel of death and destruction, an agent of Satan.

From a lowly backwoods attorney, through his use as a clever scribbler and accomplished debater with phenomenal oratorical skills, Abraham Lincoln elevated himself to the most powerful seat in the land, and from this lofty perch could rain down death and destruction upon all those who dared claim philosophical concepts of life, liberty, and property against his tyrannical views.

PASSIONS

Too much has been written with so much vehemence on the question of the morality of that institution we call "slavery," the most extreme and severest form of man's exploitation of man for financial gain. Through labored arguments and convoluted reasoning both sides strove mightily to sway the general population to their respective positions in the incessant arguments. The writings and debates, progressively more voluminous and more heated, surrendered reason to passion, fact to propaganda till it overwhelmed the South with its shrill denunciations. Unlike calm rational humans, dispassionately presenting a cerebral analysis to the table, they became possessed and blinded by their passions, ever escalating the rhetoric to the breaking point, and that was when the South put forth their own Declaration of Independence. This became unacceptable to Abraham Lincoln, who, upon becoming president with the greatest power available, resolved the issue in a most un-Christian way by butchering his fellow Americans into submission!

Out of five European powers, ten South American countries, Central America, and Mexico, only two involved violent and bloody conflict with regards to the issue of slavery.

To its eternal shame, one of these was the United States of America! The other was St. Domingue (Haiti) forever mired in its subculture of backward primitive peoples inclined to solving its difficulties violently. The other nineteen conglomerations of civilized bodies managed to "solve" the "problem" of slavery by peaceful, enlightened cerebrations. As the one and only democracy in the Western World, it becomes all the more amazing that its leadership could not control its bloodthirsty passions and lust for war to bring about a resolution to what should be considered a minor problem in the greater scheme of world affairs.

FANATICISM AND ABOLITIONISM

I particularly enjoyed writer Amos Os's definition of a fanatic in the Columbus Dispatch on March19, 2006. "He (the fanatic) wants to save your soul: he wants to redeem you; he wants to liberate you from sin, from error, from smoking, from your faith or faithlessness; he wants to inspire your eating habits or cure you of your drinking or voting habits." It implies, but not adequately conveys, the crazed, monomaniacal fervor of these people. Blinded by their passions they would kill you to save you! I refer of course to the abolitionist's rabid pursuit to end slavery in America by causing the Civil War, which led to the brutal butchering of all those connected with this odious industry. To them the death of over 1,000,000 people is an insignificant footnote in the panorama of history. Blasphemy!

In some discussions on the issue of abolitionism, it sometimes describes altruistically as the first civil rights movement. Others might say simply it was "the right thing to do." Little do they seem to care for the big picture. Little do they care to analyze the potential consequences of their actions. They care not to look beyond their noses as to what might happen from their behavior. They find total solace in their altruism, misguided though it may be. They find total justification in the catchphrase "If it feels good, do it!"

HISTORY OF SLAVERY

All throughout history from the dawn of civilization to the twenty-first century, we can find the existence of what we are now told is reprehensible behavior, slavery! In our studies we find it was an integral part of the ancient Egyptian, Greek, and Roman civilizations and, when it is discussed in the Bible, all references are positive and benign. Never is it referred as a sin nor as an abomination. It was merely a fact of life, a normal and accepted part of their civilization. In America, the first slaves to be introduced were by the Spanish settlers in St. Augustine, Florida, in 1581. The first slaves in English America were twenty slaves into Jamestown, Virginia, in 1619. Thus, even in America, slavery has a long and relatively benign existence, and the question arises: why did slavery become such a hot button issue in the mid-1800s?

The Roman aristocrat Cato described his farm tools into three categories (1) the voiceless (wagons and plows), (2) the inarticulate (oxen and mules), and (3) the speaking (slaves). So too the Southern aristocrats might have defined their "farm tools" in exactly the same manner. All were essential for the proper functioning and eventual prosperity of the plantation.

We admire and give thanks to Athens for giving us the concepts of democracy but less so because they maintained slavery *throughout its existence* (and never granted political rights to women). Was it because slavery was considered *no big deal?* For about 200 years, the United States was similar to Athens in that slavery coexisted with democracy, and it was only when the troublemaking abolitionists put it in our heads that slavery was a big deal that the nation was persuaded (at least the northern half) that the practice was reprehensible and incompatible with the moral precepts of democracy. The catastrophe that is euphemistically called the American Civil War was the result of these machinations.

And now we turn our attention to the twenty-first century where we observe a modern-day evolution of "slavery" in the industry we call "human trafficking" for it includes all the classic elements traditionally associated with slavery—abduction, false promises, transportation to a strange place, loss of freedom, abuse, violence, and deprivation.

SLAVERY AND THE BIBLE

When the colonies broke free from the mother country, Britain, an interesting consequence is that America split itself not only on North and South political, economic, and social lines but also on North and South interpretations of Christian doctrine. The South was inclined to believe that words had meaning and, through a literal, interpretation of the Bible concluded that because nothing in the Old Testament condemned slavery, it was, therefore, sanctioned. The great patriarch Abraham, as well as other notables had slaves with apparently God's blessings. Solomon built the temple with slave labor. Neither Jesus nor the Apostles uttered a word against slavery and slaveholders, much less declared it sinful.

Notwithstanding the black and white support for slavery, the radical abolitionists and some prominent clergymen, could and did, with tunnel vision, ignore the facts. With impunity they emphasized the superiority of the spirit of the Bible over the Word as a major consideration in their discussions over slavery. Guided by their conscience in interpreting Christian doctrine they argued for humanitarianism and benevolence as God's central essence. Modern-day slavery was declared as incompatible with Christian practice, attacking slavery and slaveholders as anti-Christ and, therefore, sinful. Repeatedly, they argued they were being guided by a "higher law" (than the Bible?!) and all actions became thoroughly justified.

Some even had the arrogance and audacity, verging on heresy and blasphemy, to insist that, if the Bible could be shown to sanction slavery, it should be discarded as the devil's own work. Even Lincoln is said to have uttered, "If slavery is not wrong, nothing is wrong." Infected by this spirit of Democracy, now religion, as well as politics, could be open to individual and different interpretations. In this environment everyone was free to judge, not only the Constitution but also all facets of Christian doctrine. They could deny that biblical words had meaning and, ironically, could also deny Southern states rights clearly articulated in the Constitution!

Ordinarily, to counter the written facts as found in the Bible, a logical argument against slavery would require feats of mental gymnastics and dishonesty of an unprecedented nature.

Unable to find scriptural support for their premises in an attempt to condemn slavery these radical abolitionists, in collusion with their notable clerics, had to resort to chicanery of the most blatant variety. By cleverly insisting that Christian compassion and humanitarianism superseded and trumped all logic, declaring slavery incompatible with modern-day Christian practice!

They concluded, therefore, that slavery was an abomination in the eyes of God, a sinful practice to be eradicated from the world by whatever means necessary. Even after all the dust had settled and the 1,000,000 bodies buried, no one paused to contemplate the horrendous consequences of their actions stemming from being moved by the spirit of the Bible! The rallying cry for the North should not have been "Save the Union" but "I kill you in the name of Jesus."

SIN

The concept of sin was originally and primarily a religious one; it is the transgression of the law of God and an offence against God. But Lincoln modified and muddied this interpretation to suit his present condition by calling it a moral flaw. In either case this "sin" deserves punishment and calls down the righteous wrath of God upon the slave holders, masters, and sellers. The American Civil War was America's Armageddon, the final engagement between good and evil. Here Lincoln usurped God's righteous and divine wrath, becoming God's agent on earth, at times being a loving and forgiving God, at others, as here, an angry, vengeful one punishing man to bring him to repentance.

SLAVERY AND THE BIBLE

There exist many Civil War historians who remained adamant in their assertion that slavery was not the major issue in causing the confrontation between the North and the South. Allow me to throw cold water upon this preposterous assertion and disabuse the reader of this bullshit directly by quoting a line from the horse's mouth. Upon meeting Harriet Beecher Stowe for the first time in the White House, Abraham Lincoln uttered these profoundly revealing words: "So this is the lady who wrote that book that caused this great war." By doing so, Lincoln admitted to all the world, despite many protestations to the contrary, that *slavery* indeed became the monster avalanche that careened out of control causing the enormous death, destruction, and desolation that we know as the Civil War! It was without a doubt *the* cause of the Civil War!

In construction of their position, the abolitionists and their fellow travelers needed a plausible and convincing argument to justify intrusion and interference with this institution.

Beginning with simple statements that slavery was an abomination, and adding more and more similar, but progressively more vehement and strident urgings, they finally struck the mother lode of responsive cords in the Christian community. The frequent repetition with convincing zeal that slavery was a sin in the eyes, of God created the propaganda coup of the nineteenth century and perhaps for all time by brainwashing the American populace as to its veracity! Because these accusations were made by respected leaders of the Christian community they surely must be accepted as Gospel truth, and all Christians must act to remedy and rectify this abhorrent situation!

However, there is one major fly in this ointment. If, as it has been often said that, the nineteenth century inhabitants had an astonishingly total command of the Old Testament, the question arises: why did they conveniently ignore it? For if we look at the Bible, Old and New Testaments, we find that nowhere can be found any condemnation, or even negative reference, regarding this well-established institution, slavery! Nowhere! Yet this is the basis of all the friction and heat between the North and South brethren! It does not take a careful study by scholars or historians that the Bible reveals slavery to be a normal occurrence in the Middle East, and the rules, laws, and other regulations regarding slaves were designed and considered essential to stability and social order. Even during the time of the Vikings, AD 980–1009, Dublin was a major slave-trading center where tens of thousands of Irish, Scots, and Anglo-Saxons were bought and sold.

COMMENTS ON SLAVERY IN THE BIBLE OLD TESTAMENT

In Genesis 37:28, Joseph's brothers sold him into slavery to the Ishmaelites for twenty pieces of silver. It is characterized as an event of minor reprehensibility, just a betrayal by his brothers. Yet the abolitionists in the 1800s magnified such behavior as an abomination and in the eyes of God. It was not so characterized in the Bible.

Exodus 1:11 The Egyptians under a new king made slaves of the Israelites.

Exodus 21:2 Laws concerning Hebrew slaves

:2 If you buy a Hebrew slave, he shall serve only 6 years and be freed on the seventh year, and need not pay anything to regain his freedom.

:3 If he sold himself as a slave before he married, then if he married afterward only he shall be freed; but if he was married before he became a slave, then his wife shall be freed with him at the same time. But if his master gave him a wife while he was a slave, and they have sons and daughters, the wife and children shall still belong to the master, and he shall go out by himself free.

Leviticus 25:44 However, you may purchase slaves from foreign nations living around you, and you may purchase the children of the foreigners living among you, eventhough they have been born in our land. They will be permanent slaves for you to pass on to your children after you.

Deuteronomy 15:12 If you buy a Hebrew slave, whether man or woman, you must free him at the end of the sixth year you have owned him.

NEW TESTAMENT

Romans 1:1 This letter is from Paul, Jesus Chris's slave chosen to be a missionary and went out to preach God's Good News.

Ephesians 6:5 Slaves, obey your masters, be eager to give them your best. Serve them as you would Christ. Don't work hard only when your master is watching and then shirk when he is not looking work hard with gladness all the time, as though working for Christ, doing the work of God with all our hearts. Remember, the Lord will pay on for each good thing you do whether you are slave or free, and you slave owners must treat your slaves right, just as I have told them to treat you. Don't keep threatening them; remember you yourselves are slaves to Christ; you have the same master they do, and He has no favorites.

Colossians 3:22 You slaves must always obey your earthly masters.
4:1 You slave owners must be just and fair to all your slaves.

THE ROLE OF RELIGION AND SLAVERY

In the voluminous writings on slavery, much emphasis has been placed on the role of religion in bringing about the end of the odious process in America and throughout the world. Based upon the idealized concept that most world religions give value to the individual person and to their presence here, many religious leaders were also in the forefront in the efforts in working for the end of the slave trade and for the abolition of slavery itself. Besides their open campaigns in public and the press, noisily and vociferously attacking the Southern aristocrats, they also secretly assisted slaves to escape from their masters and, once free, they used the Underground Railroad to conduct them to the tentative freedom north of the Ohio River and to the absolute freedom in Canaan (Canada). Runaways, especially after the Fugitive Slave Act was passed in 1850, were still in jeopardy of being tracked down and returned South to their masters, but not if they made it to Canada.

My criticism of the Christians' activities in bringing about the abolition of slavery is twofold. Almost without exception when history books talk about the Quakers it is with a reverential tone as they wax eloquently, almost breathlessly, in admiration of their principled stance on the issue of slavery. I single out the Quakers because of their claim to moral supremacy resulting from their concept of nonviolence. Having succeeded in promoting and electing Abraham Lincoln, their moral outrage seemed to have become strangely silent, or nonexistent, as he went about the savage business of butchering, and in turn being butchered by, the South. Where was their anger as Lincoln trashed their moral foundation? Why did they not speak out and rail against this moral outrage against their basic tenets? Instead they stood idly by, deaf and dumb, as the devastation engulfed them for four years of bitter fratricide! Their moral outrage had the stench of hypocritical selectivity!

DEBATE: CHRISTIANITY, THE BIBLE, SLAVERY

Historical text books are replete with the raging debates between proslavery and antislavery factions, each quoting the Bible to buttress their respective positions. If the messages were not clear, personal interpretations were used to support their side and refute their opponents. Obfuscation became their watchword. How could it be that the same book read by so many people could support such diametrically opposite views? A certain elasticity in their argumentation can be found, i.e., "If it is not specifically forbidden then it must be allowed," or "if it is not specifically allowed, it must be forbidden." Where the Bible remained silent, opportunistic assumptions could and would be made, for surely an all-good, all-powerful God would not permit evil, injustice, and suffering to exist in this world! Using this line of reasoning, proponents of abolition could convincingly make any argument possible to substantiate their assertion as to the evil nature of slavery! Theirs was an obedience to a "higher law," higher than man's inferior attempts to control man's behavior.

Sermon after sermon, article after article, book after book, debate after debate raged back and forth, each side claiming to possess the ultimate truth in the matter, escalating step by step in vehemence and passion leading to an avalanche of insults and ceaseless provocations culminating in the slaughter of Americans in the Civil War, an unmitigated disaster! Slavery versus freedom would no longer be debated and decided with words but by the imposition of one man's iron, uncompromising will. Blood and steel, the stench of gunpowder and rotting flesh would assail the nostrils and decide the issue once and for all!

It is amazing to me that, in a purported Christian nation as the United States claims to be, the admonition in one of Moses's Ten Commandments, "Thou shalt not kill," seems to have been overlooked. Is it the "thou"; is it the "shalt"; is it the "not"; or is it the "kill" that they have difficulty with and not completely understand? Even I, as an atheist, have no difficulty understanding! What Christians! What hypocrisy! Was their battle cry, I kill you in the name of Jesus Christ for your unforgiveable sin of slavery?

The abolitionists rationalized the contradictory statements of the

Bible regarding slavery by asserting the Declaration of Independence to be the "secular version of American scripture" and that this document unambiguously was for abolition. In their minds these liberal values eventually won out, justifying their extreme treatment of the South in pursuit of these noble objectives. These callous people, including the subsequent historians, casually swept under the rug, out of sight and out of mind, the brutal fact of the horrendous expenditure involved the deaths of over 1,000,000 Americans and billions of dollars for the destruction, North and South. This cavalier attitude is reminiscent of a later tyranny, Joseph Stalin who is quoted as having said; "One death is a tragedy, but a million is only a statistic." To do terrible things for a "righteous cause" and come away feeling good about it stems from an arrogance and feeling of self-importance on an unprecedented scale. To them the murder of over 1,000,000 Americans is the "lesser evil" than the enslavement of four million Africans. In the minds of even the casual Christians does this mentality not verge on hypocrisy or even worse blasphemy? Thus, the death of the single individual, Abraham Lincoln, is portrayed as a tragedy, but the deaths of over 1,000,000 American soldiers is mere statistic!

SHOCKING THE CONSCIENCE

Is my conscience the only one in the whole United States to be shocked to its foundation by the unconscionable attitude of the abolitionists, the majority of the citizens of the North, and especially by those who should know better, the historians, by the horrendous number of young American men slaughtered on the fields of battle in the American Civil War? History textbooks tell us that over 1,000,000 brave American souls were interred in American soil yet Abraham Lincoln is portrayed as one of our greatest presidents and the Civil War was a noble enterprise. If there is such a thing as secular blasphemy then this is it!

SLAVERY AND RELIGION

History books tell us of that phenomenon called the Great Awakening of the 1730s and the 1740s, essentially a religious revival reaction to the prevailing rationalism and formalism and then there was the Second Great Awakening of the 1790s. In religiously oriented texts, they are described as "spontaneous works of the Holy Spirit, visitations of God's grace for the renewal of America's sacred mission." The Second moreover, laid an emphasis on "usefulness," which led to attacks on such social ills as slavery, sexism, poverty, prostitution, alcoholism, and war. Logically, one would expect that these expressions of frenzied spiritual activity would lead to a greater study of the Bible and a better awareness of its teachings. With regards to the issue of slavery, there seems to be little evidence to substantiate such a preposition. Where the Bible treats slavery as a matter-of-fact institution, these zealots fabricated a viewpoint that the Bible regarded slavery as an unmitigated evil, an abomination in the eyes of God, and therefore, a sin. Virtually all references in the Bible on the subject of slavery contradict such a bald-faced lie and assertion

RELIGIOUS OPPOSITION TO SLAVERY

As early as 1688, four Quakers in Pennsylvania declared their opposition to slavery in what became known as the Germantown Protest. Without biblical support or reference they put forth their own philosophical worldview as to what is good or what is bad. "If slavery was good, what can we say is… evil. There is a saying, that we should do to all men like as we will be done ourselves; making no difference of what generation, descent, or colour they are." In 1693, Quaker George Keith printed the first antislavery tract in the English Colonies, "An Exhortation and Caution to Friends Concerning Buying or Keeping of

Negroes." He urge them to free their own slaves, work against slavery, and help fugitive slaves. Quaker John Woolman took it upon himself to warn their fellows of "divine wrath unless they abolished slavery immediately." Samuel Sewell's 1700 tract charged that any man who held another enslaved had "forfeited a great part of his own claim to humanity."

The antislavery movement took a prolonged sabbatical for it was not until 1758–1774 that Pennsylvania Quakers severed all connections with the international slave trade and demanded that all members in good faith free their slaves.

Where did the abolitionists acquire this mania to free the slaves, this idealism, this truly profound philosophical conviction, this morality? If they claimed to be responding to a "higher law" then their explanation is in direct contrast and contradiction to these passages from the Bible. Is this not blasphemy? Yet they do use the Bible to suit their own ends whenever it is convenient. They use the biblical reference of "how the children of Israel were delivered out of Egypt from bondage" to buttress their argument against slavery.

What could have possessed Ralph Waldo Emerson to make such a blasphemous comment when he referred to John Brown's execution."Who, if he shall suffer (execution) will make the gallows glorious like the cross." Or Julia Ward Howe when she made the Christian parallel in her Battle Hymn of the Republic. "As He died to make men holy, let us die to make men free while God is marching on." More accurately is she not saying "let us kill to make men free" and thereby breaking most emphatically one of God's Ten Commandments, "Thou shalt not kill." Such blatant heresy seems to have gone un-noticed by the Christian community!

Then there is the utterances of another supposedly knowledgeable Christian, Theodore Parker, when he authoritatively said, "Whatever laws men made to perpetuate the ownership of one man by another, the supreme law, made by God, forbade the practice?! And the law of God must always take precedence over the law of man."

ABOLITIONISTS

Many of the abolitionists were Quakers and conscientious objectors who were opposed to war, seemingly paragons of moral rectitude, but that did not prevent them from being agitators and provocateurs. Like a drunken crowd watching a barroom brawl they could claim to be above the altercation as participants but that did not stop them from being vociferous eggers-on from the safety of the bleachers. Go get him, Abe! He's a son-of-a-bitch slaveholder, a miserable bastard, scum of the earth. Bite his nose off! Gouge his eyes out! Kill him!

CHRISTIANITY AND THE ABOLITIONIST MOVEMENT

Christians are insistent that Christianity has shaped the core values and institutions of the United States and the west and has fostered in our civilization values such as respect for human dignity, human rights, and equality; equality because we have been created so in the eyes of God. They boast that movements to abolish slavery occurred only in the West and led by Christians. First, the Quakers and then the evangelical Christians demanded that since we are all equal in God's eyes, no man has a right to rule another man without his consent. This religious doctrine, in addition for giving the moral justification for ending slavery, is the fundamental enunciation of democratic governance! The idea of self-government is also rooted in the Christian assumption of human equality.

Never mind that the Bible makes no disparaging or critical remarks on the issue of slavery. Never mind that the Bible tells us of the ubiquitous and common practice and presence of slavery in biblical times in both the Egyptian, Greek, and Roman civilizations. Never mind that that slavery was understood and well-tolerated with certain and definite rules and regulations regarding conduct and treatment of slaves. This, however, did not stop the Christians in the early 1800s to campaign for the abolition of slavery on their own initiative and without concrete support, insisting that it (slavery) was a sin in the eyes of God. The rest is blood-soaked history as, once the dogs of war were loosed, the carnage could not be stopped until virtual total annihilation of the South occurred.

Religion: Lincoln's call to national prayer were frequent and profound, yet all the while he could urge his troops to butcher and pillage the South in the name of Jesus Christ and all humanity.

QUAKERS AND THE ABOLITION OF SLAVERY

A surprising finding, if one is aware and pays attention to one's reading, is the fact that many Quakers were in the forefront of the abolitionist movement. One of these is Benjamin Lundy (1789–1839) who, in 1815, organized the Abolitionist Union Humane Society, and from 1822–1824 published "The Genius of Universal Emancipation" a small monthly paper devoted exclusively to the abolition of slavery.

In reading about the Quakers in various texts and sources they are described as "a mystical reform movement known for their humanitarianism." "They studied the Bible but did not accept it as the only rule of faith and practice" and "even rejected the Bible as the basis for Church authority." They are known for "rejection of formality in worship and belief in creeds." Also they were known for their "denunciation of all creeds and ecclesiastical customs as well as political and economic conventions." They preferred to follow the "inner light of Christ that dwells in the hearts of ordinary people," this "divine immediate revelation within to the authority of the church, creed or Bible."

Therefore, in their zeal to abolish slavery the Quakers followed the guidance if this "inner light," which they considered a higher? Moral guidance than the Bible yet no one was critical of this point of view with in most Christian circles would be judged as blasphemy! To the truly believing Christian community nothing is superior to the Bible! To them slavery was incompatible with this consciencelike energy that emanated from their souls when the mind was in a state of contemplation and repose. This "inner light" was the guiding principle in man's behavior toward his fellow man. Therefore, to them, slavery must be abolished now!

But, once the dogs of war were let loose, there was no stopping the carnage through this miscalculation of horrendous impact. There would be no simple ninety day war for the ninety-day enlistees. The superiority in armaments and numbers were insufficient to crush a determined, well-led force galvanized to repulse this "foreign" army invading their home soil! And during all the four years of death destruction and carnage the "inner light" of the Quakers seemed to be considerable dimmed, if not totally extinguished. Where was their Christian outrage then?

Much has been made of the interesting observation that Abraham Lincoln filled his cabinet with political opponents and through the force of his personality shaped them for the difficult tasks ahead. The post of Secretary of War was filled by a man sensitive to the sufferings of black slavery, an antislavery Quaker by the name of Edwin M. Stanton, who by his actions belied the long-established view that Quakers were fiercely pacifists. We are told they reject war and military service, that they stress peace and education, and that they devoutly follow God's will. Yet Stanton became a most ruthless and bloodthirsty war secretary always ready to urge the most severe measures be taken against the rebels.

QUAKERS

I object to the special considerations and deference given to the Quakers, and their like-minded brethren, in all the literature, ascribing to them an undeserved respect for their piousness and religiosity. Their ascetic lives are revered by all as a manifestation of their strict obedience to the Bible.

In the battle against slavery they were undoubtedly first and foremost in their persistent efforts to abolish this odious institution, first in England then in the New World. According to them, it was an article of faith that all individuals possessed a divine inner light that made slavery a sin against God. Apparently they did not consult the teachings of the Bible in this matter but made it up by and for themselves. Nowhere, nowhere does the Bible remonstrate against slavery! This institution was a matter-of-fact occurrence in Egyptian, Greek, and Roman civilizations, and in biblical times, accepted and tolerated, with kindly suggestions to be benevolent to the slaves. By missing this important fact we must conclude two things: either the abolitionists were woefully ignorant of this discussion in the Bible or they deliberately chose to ignore its teachings to push forward their own agenda. In either case their concerted efforts contributed greatly to precipitating America's bloodiest and deadliest carnage—the American Civil War—where they should be found guilty for causing the deaths of 1,000,000 soldiers and over 20,000 civilians!

All the abolitionists, including Harriet Beecher Stowe, lie smugly in and snugly their graves confident that they were instrumental in the noble cause in emancipating 4 million Negroes from slavery, all the while denying that their actions contributed to the deaths of over 1,000,000 Americans (North and South).

QUAKERS

In the April 2007 issue of American History Magazine, on page 28, the author makes an interesting statement: "The Quakers troubled him (Roger Williams) both politically and religiously, especially because he was convinced that they elevated themselves above Scripture and paid no heed to conventional manners and morality." If memory serves me right a significant number of Lincoln's cabinet, including Lincoln, had Quaker family influence. Thus, in my humble opinion, an argument can be made, and perhaps a book can be written, of the disproportionate influence by this minor sect had upon American and, thus, world, affairs. As a purported antiwar, nonbelligerent, peaceful people, history reveals their mind-boggling major influence in instigating and precipitating this American Holocaust. Christianity has a lot of explaining to do. For instance, what does "Thou shalt not kill" mean?

HIGHER LAW

From even before the colonists landed on these shores, they were noted for being heavily steeped in the traditions of Christianity relying on and mainly guided by the Bible as the ultimate source of morality, a rule book on Christianity. The Ten Commandments alone are sufficient guideposts for the obedient Christian to lead them safely through all the trials and vicissitudes on this earthly existence. However, this assumption seems to have escaped the attention of the abolitionists who, despite the benign assessment of slavery in the Bible, took it upon themselves to discover a "higher law" with regards to this issue here and now in America. Is it not blasphemous for any professed Christian to claim or make any assertion that their opinion supersedes the Bible? From their assertion that "if slavery is not wrong, nothing is wrong" they make a nonsyllogistic argument that, in essence, justifies their defiance of the Bible and the laws of America and assert their right to abolish this evil institution—slavery!

For them the emotional concept of "human rights" trumps all forms of logic and claims superiority over all forms of rational construction. The Bible, having no proscription against slavery, and indeed defends the institution, is a major impediment that must be ignored! This "higher law" does that! The abolitionists, supposed pillars of the Christian community, even go so far as to ignore that inconvenient proscription "Thou shalt not kill" as an outdated concept in this modern day and age. Thus, the butchery of over 600,000 Americans in that holocaust known as the American Civil War, is justifiable homicide in pursuit of that noble goal: emancipation of the slaves. To kill the slave owner, the overseer, the trader, and all who support them was a noble endeavor, worthy of heroic recognition. They were the ultimate arbiters of morality for the new nation. The deaths of over 600,000 Americans was merely a statistic to be overlooked and ignored.

ABOLITIONISTS

The preeminence of Christianity in the abolition of slavery is apparent to even the casual history student. In England, the activity of John Wesley (1703–1791) is famous not only for developing the evangelical form of Christianity known as Methodism but also for the abolition of slavery; in 1774 he published a tract "Thoughts on Slavery." In a letter to William Wilberforce he urged the former to devote himself to the antislavery campaign as a "glorious enterprise" that opposed "that execrable villainy which is the scandal of religion, of England, and of human nature."

During nearly all of his political career, Wilberforce harangued the British parliament, and eventually succeeded in bringing about the abolition of the slave trade (in 1807), and the entire institution of slavery (in 1833 shortly after his death). The notion that good works and charity, being essential components of the Christian life, became the driving force in Wilberforce's thinking and zeal in his relentless pursuit of abolition. Subsequently, on the Americas, abolition of slavery can also be viewed as a uniquely Christian endeavor. Foremost in the struggle were the Quakers, Harriet Beecher Stowe, Frederick Douglass, William Lloyd Garrison, the Methodists, and others of the Christian community.

Whereas the British abolition, perhaps as a reflection of British restraint, rectitude, and civilized behavior, contrasts diametrically with that of the Americas, for it was virtually bloodless. The American effort, on the other hand, seemed more in keeping with the wild, untamed, and uncivilized nature of the country for their abolition was a bitter divisive Civil War in which passions ruled over reason, brute force trumped rational discussion and compromise. Its leaders did not have the grueling patience for diplomacy, a process of give and take that characterizes a civilized society instead took the no-brainer course of brute force.

The movie "Amazing Grace" is a noble presentation of a noble person in a noble cause, whereas an accurate movie on Lincoln would show an impatient tyrannical butcher that he truly was, despite all the clever bullshit to the contrary. All the historians persist in portraying him as the savior of the Union, all the while neglecting the horrendous price paid in human lives.

WILLIAM WILBERFORCE (1759–1833)

The movie "Amazing Grace" is a remarkable dramatization of the political life of William Wilberforce in his long crusade against the slave trade and slavery itself in Great Britain. With dogged persistence he, year after year, introduced bills in the House of Commons to abolish slavery, and year after year his bills failed. Much of this was due to the fact that many of the members of Parliament had financial interests in slavery and saw no reason to vote against their (and the crown's) financial interests declaring that if they did not participate in the slave trade, it would be taken over by their arch rivals, the French. One member (in the movie) summed it up very nicely by saying: "This great ship of state must not be sunk by a wave of good intentions." Nevertheless, after many years of persistence, perseverance, and gradualism, the British parliament finally voted to abolish the slave trade!

William Wilberforce is sometimes referred to as the "Great Christian emancipator," whose long, arduous, and perhaps most importantly bloodless, efforts persuaded the British parliament to finally abolish slavery in Britain and all its possessions. This is in stark contradistinction to Abraham Lincoln who can be truthfully labeled the "great non- or pseudo-Christian emancipator" and who also succeeded in bringing about the abolition of slavery in America, not through patient persuasion and negotiation but by brutal bloody conquest of the South. Yet Lincoln is remembered as the greater luminary! Preposterous.

Historians and related image-makers have carefully crafted an image of Abraham Lincoln as a kind, benevolent humanitarian who would not harm a fly, yet the facts tell a different story that most observers and students of the man seemingly have deliberately ignored and glossed over. While Dom Pedro II ascended the Brazilian throne in 1840, half the seven million Brazilians were slaves, and through his leadership *all* were freed, without a single shot being fired! How can it be that a relatively backward country could find a way to free their slaves without bloodshed while a supposedly advanced and sophisticated America regressed to barbarism and bloodshed to achieve a similar outcome? It was all about calm, cerebral leadership or lack thereof.

ELECTION

LINCOLN'S MANDATE

When history books present Abraham Lincoln's dilemma in dealing with the crisis between the North and South, it is invariably couched in noble terms, i.e., as stark choices between freedom and slavery, unity and disunion, and war and peace. Logically and emotionally the world would most certainly opt for freedom over slavery, unity over division, and most emphatically peace over war! Deep down in his soul, Lincoln insists he would have preferred a peaceful resolution to the impasse, yet when war looms its ugly head, he offers up the weak excuse that it was thrust upon him by powerful external forces and that he did not have any other recourse but to wage war upon the recalcitrant South. This is a preposterous evasion of his moral responsibility as president to actively and aggressively pursue every avenue that might lead to a peaceful resolution. The art of diplomacy, of negotiation and compromise, requires the enormous expenditure of effort and energy to achieve a resolution that, however imperfect, avoids the butchery that is euphemistically called the American Civil War. Lincoln, instead of being worshipped as the Savior of the country, should be castigated and vilified for his abject failure at statesmanship, surrendering instead to the forces of common political expediency and barbarism.

In the election of 1860 that pitted Abraham Lincoln against his arch rival Northern Democrat Stephen A. Douglas, the Union Part's John Bell, and Southern Democrat John C. Breckenridge, Lincoln received 39.8% of the 4,689,568 votes cast. Even the most partisan Lincoln supporter must admit that this plurality, not majority, is hardly the *sufficient mandate* that would compel any leader to embark upon the murderous rampage that was the American Civil War and then have the audacity to characterize it as a noble crusade and justifiable homicide. By insisting that America was a sacrosanct, inviolable Union he would allow the slaughter of over 1,000,000 Americans to prevent its dissolution and prove his point! That is the tragedy of it all!

Lincoln: 1,865,593 votes Douglas: 1,382,713 votes
Breckenridge: 848,356 votes Bell: 592,906 votes

Yet we have writers who deliberately attempt to mislead and confuse us by concentrating on the electoral vote and not the popular vote. One writer wrote, "He won the 1860 election with a comfortable electoral cushion" and he won a second term "capturing all but three states for a 212-12 electoral landslide."

LINCOLN'S ELECTION

Apart from George Washington's ascendency to the throne of the first president of the United States of America by the anointing by a grateful nation, all subsequent seekers of this office competed fiercely and vigorously, sometimes viciously and bitterly for this great prize. The competition between John Adams and Thomas Jefferson was the first example of the spirited activity for this seat of preeminence that caused a bruising of egos and sensibilities of both candidates.

By the time of Abraham Lincoln the political forces in the nation, having become more sophisticated and devious in their actions, knew how to handicap and prepare their horses for the races to come. In smoke-filled rooms away from the prying public eyes their machinations took place, as they plotted, planned, and schemed with all the appropriate give and take that is required in these circles, to elevate this dark-horse candidate, a backwoods lawyer and almost full-time politician into a respectable possibility for the presidency. Having achieved a favorable exposure in the nation's newspapers through his widely publicized debates with Stephen Douglas, his stance on the issue of Slavery attracted him to powerful political and wealthy Bostonians. With the abolitionists they felt that the issue of slavery was a distinct threat to the American way of life but more so to their financial interests, even their existence. It was, therefore, imperative for them to act and to act quickly to support this slavery opponent. Once they put him into the white house, he could do their dirty work for him as their exclusive puppet.

It is instructive to remember Lord Acton who uttered that memorable comment on the political process, "Power tends to corrupt and absolute power corrupts absolutely. Great men are almost always bad men. There is no worse heresy than that the office sanctifies the holder of it." Lincoln was a glaring example of what Lord Acton was referring to. Sufficient evidence exists in the history books revealing the existence of a "great left-wing conspiracy" and the use of "dirty tricks" in the election of Abraham Lincoln to the Presidency. A dispassionate, critical analysis of the Republican Convention in Chicago clearly shows what I am talking about.

BEHIND THE SCENES: LINCOLN SUPPORTERS

William Henry Herndon, Lincoln's friend and law partner and biographer wrote: "No man ever had an easier time of it in his early days than Lincoln. He had… influential and financial friends to help him; they almost fought each other for the privilege of assisting him… Lincoln was a pet… in this city… he deserved it."

MAJOR SUPPORTERS

Joseph Medill
Impelled by his overwhelming desires to voice his opinions and influence others Medill got into the newspaper business specifically for this purpose. From a small newspaper, the Coshocton (Ohio) Whig in 1849, he parlayed this cash cow into larger more influential organs to voice his strong antislavery views. Stepping up his next bought the Cleveland Leader to campaign for a new antislavery political party. Then with Charles Ray, an editor from Galena, Illinois, they bought the Chicago Daily Tribune. Writing hard-hitting and influential editorials for this greater audience, Medill was instrumental in persuading many to back the antislavery dark horse Abraham Lincoln in his debates with Stephen Douglas in their race for the U.S. Senate in 1858. (Douglas won, but that only prodded Medill even more to work in smoke-filled rooms in Chicago to advance Lincoln for the presidency and featuring a barrage of pro-Lincoln editorials in the influential Chicago Press and Tribune beginning with a three-foot editorial headed by "The Winning Man, Abraham Lincoln" on the day before the convention came to order.

IMAGE MAKERS AND KINGMAKER

We seem to be of the impression that the mind-manipulating techniques of New York's Madison Avenue, a street where many advertising and public-relations offices reside, are of recent origin. It was here that the high pressure techniques of the advertising and image-making business became highly polished and fine-tuned. But if we look back at the political life of Abraham Lincoln we find, surprisingly, or perhaps not so surprisingly, clever manipulations of the electorate by portraying Lincoln as a man of the people… a man of humble origins, and rode this image all the way to the White House. Although Lincoln detested "Abe" as too hickish, he also recognized its appeal to the masses especially if "honest" preceded it. "Rail-splitter" was another sobriquet ingeniously begun by his cousin John Hanks at the state convention in Decatur in 1860 when a large banner tied between two fence rails and reading "Abraham Lincoln the Rail Candidate for President" and the orchestrated delegates whooped and flung their hats into the air.

KINGMAKER

In the many historical accounts concerning Marcus Alonzo "Mark" Hanna of Cleveland, concerning his clandestine activities on behalf of his man William McKinley, many of the historians are quick to point out salient pejorative aspects of his maneuverings. Some elections are "stolen" on election day with clandestine manipulations and chicanery. Others are stolen in smoke-filled rooms by power brokers in the nominating process of conventioneering but far from the scrutiny of prying eyes. Purists criticize the clandestine nature of these kingmakers secretly plotting behind the scenes in smoke-filled rooms conniving how to elevate their candidate in the eyes of the electorate. Wheeling and dealing, they put a positive spin on their candidate while minimizing his deficiencies, but also careful to attack their opponent by enlarging his deficiencies and drawbacks.

Yet in virtually all the accounts of activities by "special interest groups" on behalf of Abraham Lincoln nary is heard a disparaging word. Historians conveniently avert their critical gazes or even turn a blind eye to the shenanigans and suspicious dealings by these back-room manipulators. Not even one historian has the fortitude to even hint of any impropriety; it has been handed down that all the activities of these supporters is normal, acceptable and legitimate on behalf of "their man." His background and philosophical utterances have made Abraham Lincoln the ideal man for their purposes. All the history books would have you believe Lincoln's election was ordained in heaven with the explicit purpose of rectifying the heinous crime against humanity… the imposition and perpetuation of the "sin of sins"… slavery! Further no one dares point out that *nowhere* does the *Bible* make even a hint of an odious reference regarding slavery. It is quite safe to conclude therefore, that slavery, despite all the verbiage from the abolitionists, was *not* a sin! Yet in their efforts to correct this nonexistent sin they, and all their Northern accomplices, did commit murder, and that as we all are fully aware is most definitely a sin! Am I the only one to notice this? You would think that these facts would lead the professional historians to reassess and rethink their positions and opinions of the man in the whole panorama of what was the American Civil War.

KINGMAKERS: LINCOLN'S CONVENTION NOMINATION

Much as with "Tippecanoe" there were orchestrated vast meetings, torchlight processions with emblematic standards flying high (reminiscent of the brainwashing techniques used to great effect by one Adolf Hitler). Great speeches were part of the menu all extolling the virtues of the candidate.

Lincoln, once having earned his living splitting rails, had the benefit of the clever public relations and advertising type people long before Madison Avenue became famous for such manipulations of the masses. Together with painting rails on many decorative insignias they trained many attendees to bellow "Rail Splitter" at every opportunity at the convention.

On May 16, 1860, 40,000 strangers and 500 delegates were brought to Chicago by train thanks to Norman B. Judd, attorney for the Rock Island Railroad, who fixed it with all the railroads to allow low excursion rates for Lincoln supporters to jam the Wigwam. In combination with William Hill Lamon, who went to the printers of seat tickets, and together with a staff of young men, signed these tickets so that only Lincoln supporters could jam the hall, thereby leaving no room for Seward supporters. Then there was Judge David Davis, known as the prime behind-the-scenes orchestrator, manager and manipulator, who got the Pennsylvania delegation's support by promising Head of Treasury to Simon Cameron.

Medill of the Tribune approached Carter of Ohio, "If you can throw in the Ohio delegation for Lincoln, Chase can have anything he wants." "H-how d-dye know?" stuttered Carter. Medill answering, "I know, and you know I wouldn't promise if I didn't know."

A reporter, Murat Halstead wrote of the uproar: "Imagine all the hogs ever slaughtered in Cincinnati giving their death squeals together and a score of big steam whistles going together… the Lincoln yawp swelled into a wild hosanna of victory."

In view of the above facts it is amazing to me that no historian has ever critically commented upon, what is known in modern parlance as, "dirty tricks" that assured Lincoln's convention victory. The manipulation of the masses by the behind-the-scenes, Madison-

Avenue-type string-pullers succeeded in portraying the uproar as the spontaneous exhibition of popular support for their man Abraham Lincoln. Notwithstanding his avowals, "I authorize no bargains and will be bound by none," and "Make no contracts that will bind me," he gave full approval to his agents to do whatever was necessary to secure his nomination. He could always deny any responsibility for their actions… by these clever lawyerly escape clauses.

KINGMAKERS

Judge David Davis. Operating out of Lincoln Headquarters in the Tremont House he would send out his lieutenants Swett, Dubois, Lamon, Logan, and especially Judd, to wheel and deal with specific delegations to abandon their first choices and go with Lincoln the only candidate with the necessary credentials for victory in November. Never having held any prominent national office he, therefore, had no major enemies unlike many other candidates and held only moderate views on slavery. His speech at the Cooper Institute brought him fame and sufficient stature as to be considered presidential timber. He and his friends adroitly mailed out letters in an attempt to line up delegates in uncommitted states.

Doris Kearns Goodwin, one our nation's historians and commentators on Lincoln enumerated several elements that led to his "surprising victory" in Chicago. Among them luck, that the convention was held in his back yard and in Chicago where Lincoln enjoyed local support of all Illinois Republicans. She talked of his electability, more center of the road than any of his opponents. Instead of remarking on the "dirty tricks" that were played in Chicago she whitewashes the whole scenario by asserting that "his team played the game better than anyone else… developing the best strategy and making the right promises at the right time." He developed a camaraderie and a "band of brothers who would work for him night and day at the Chicago convention in 1860." Only a historian enraptured with the myth of Lincoln could put such a "spin," a smiley face, if you will, on an otherwise tawdry episode of political push and shove.

LINCOLN'S NOMINATION

When we think or talk about political machines, brokers, or powerful interests controlling political events where deals and plans are hatched in smoke-filled rooms, free from scrutiny by the public eye, we tend to assume this type of activity to be a twentieth century phenomenon. When, however, some historian reveals to us the existence of the Secret Six of Boston, we are led to realize that this kind of political activity flourished as early as the early 1800s. Boston, known as the hotbed of political activity from day one, was quick to realize how political power could be achieved by clandestine manipulations and thereby controlling the flow of political events to their liking.

That is how it came about that a dark horse from Illinois became the candidate from far back in the field of know quality candidates. His speech at the Cooper Institute attracted him to the powerful Eastern established interests. This speech, widely published in the press, was looked upon favorably by the general populace sufficiently to consider him presidential material. Lincoln and his friends adroitly mailed out letters in an attempt to line up delegates in uncommitted states. In the realm of propaganda the convention in Decatur, with a pre-Madison Avenue expertise, John Hanks carried a banner tied to two rotted fence rails read, "Abraham Lincoln the Rail Candidate for President in 1860." Another common theme to elevate Lincoln in the eyes of the electorate was the use of "Honest Abe," surely to appeal to the common people. Again we see a phenomenon considered also as a twentieth century invention: propaganda, the mind-manipulation of the masses adroitly used by the Northerners, most likely of New England extraction.

"In January 1860, Judd and Lincoln's Eighth Circuit chums met with him in a secret caucus and officially launched a Lincoln for President movement." "And Herndon- loyal Billy, who usually stood by Lincoln come-what-may—scoffed at his chances and dropped out of his inner circle."

As it happened, Judd had close political ties with the Chicago Tribune, which had been leaning toward Chase. But a week after Lincoln wrote Judd, the press and tribune came out for Lincoln instead, declaring him the first choice of all Illinois Republicans and exhorting them to form "Lincoln for President" clubs.

As finely run and flawlessly orchestrated an event as ever had been seen. Everything ran a precise machine because the behind-the-scenes manipulators ran the show with a tight fist.

Madison Avenue-type people would have been proud to have participated in the image-building with the portrayal of Lincoln as the "Rail Splitter" candidate and "Honest Abe" and "Humble Man of the People" orchestrating the spontaneous outpouring" for their man Lincoln. Given the long and shady history of the political machines in Chicago it is easy to conclude its origins of nefarious activities in smoke-filled rooms of the Republican Convention of 1860. Lincoln's people were as well-organized and "slick" as any king-making cabal in the history of American Politics. Many behind-the-scenes maneuverings and deal-makings took place in Chicago, some actual, others apocryphal. The most ironic was that of Judge Joseph Casey, Cameron's representative, who felt Pennsylvania would have a place in the cabinet in exchange for their votes to Lincoln. Others deny that the deal was ever uttered.

At a time when Federal senators were elected by their respective state legislatures, it is interesting to note that Abraham Lincoln was rejected on two occasions, both in 1855 and 1858. One might argue that, because he was well known by his colleagues, and by the old saying "familiarity breeds contempt," this was the reason for such an ignominious outcome. It is remarkable to note that when he is even less known by the nation, he succeeds in winning the most powerful seat in the land!

As seemingly is the case in all political conventions, much horse trading, dealing, and promising goes on with candidates facing power brokers exchanging patronage and other considerations for votes and cash. Thurlow Weed, a known prime manipulator, promised the vice-presidential nomination to the Illinois delegates if they supported Seward on the first ballot and sweetened the offer with a contribution of $100,000 to the campaign chests of the Illinois and Indiana Republican parties

Delahay, the Kansas Republican whose expenses Lincoln was paying, wrote of Lincoln that his team (Davis, Dubois, etc.) were "too honest to advance your Prospects as surely as I would like to see" in comparison with the "desperate gamblers" from New York. He suggested

Lincoln promise the full control of patronage to Pennsylvania, Iowa, Massachusetts, and Ohio for their votes. He added, "I know you have no relish for such a Game, but it is an old maxim that you must fight the *devil with fire.*"

LINCOLN, THE FRONT MAN

Despite their most ardent and aggressive efforts, the abolitionists were unable to bring about their desired results, freeing the Negro from slavery. Their aim was to elevate his status to that of the most-recently arrived laboring class immigrant. And as the immigrant he would be "entitled to the bread he earns." Political activities on the local levels did not produce the desired traction, and only stiffened Southern resistance as they felt it was a direct attack upon the very foundations of their material well-being. What they needed they found in Abraham Lincoln, a powerful orator infused with of the morally indefensible exploitation of a most primitive people and the political desire that would drive him to impose his will, if necessary, upon the nation.

With the remarkable help of experts in the field of propaganda, in smoke-filled rooms, with manipulators and string-pullers he would be elevated to heroic status, exuding honesty and integrity, so that his actions, no matter how brutal and bloody, would be eventually concluded as justifiable exertions on behalf of mankind. He would "save the nation."

That propaganda exists to this very day. Americans have a love affair with histories of people from humble beginnings through hard work and diligence reaching success in our society. Thus, from a log cabin in Kentucky, sometimes working as a "rail splitter," elevating himself (self-taught) to becoming a successful circuit-riding attorney, engaging in debates to establish his credentials as a worthy debater and possibly leader of the nation.

Lincoln articulated, as shown by his debates and speeches, the essence of what the New England factory owners were thinking—freedom for the slaves. By making them "free labor," the playing field would be leveled to that of the most recently arrived immigrants which Northern factory owners were required to use in their mills.

His handlers and manipulators were more clever and careful than the Secret Six of Boston (that secret cabal that planned and financed the lunatic John Brown's raid on Harpers Ferry). At this late juncture it would be almost impossible to identify all those who put him into the office of president and caused that tragedy of tragedies—the Civil War.

We do, however, have some evidence of a behind-the-scenes-cabal cleverly orchestrating his rise as a way-in-the back dark horse as he hurdles to the front of the pack and wins the nomination. No one in the history books is suspicious of these events leading up to his nomination at the Republican National Convention at the Wig-Wam in Chicago.

LINCOLN THE DEVIOUS

Lincoln was always very careful to repeatedly claim that the aim of the war was always "to preserve the Union" and not to end slavery. But as the debates between Lincoln and Stephen Douglas reveal the war was all about the slavery issue! Once the war was nearing a successful resolution did Lincoln feel it "right" to then issue the Emancipation Proclamation. Too late did the nation realize that they had been snookered!

DICTATOR

HOUSE DIVIDED—BIBLICAL ALLUSIONS

Matthew 7
> 24: "Therefore whosoever heareth these sayings of mine, and doeth them, I will liken him unto a wise man which built his house on a rock
> 25: And the rains descended, and the floods came, and the winds blew and beat upon the house; and it fell not: for it was founded upon a rock.
> 26: And every one that heareth these sayings of mine, and doeth not, shall be likened unto a foolish man which built his house upon the sand:
> 27: And the rain descended, and the floods came, and the rain beat upon that house; and great was the fall of it."

Matthew 12
> 25: "And Jesus knew their thoughts and said unto them, every kingdom divided against itself is brought to desolation; and every city or house divided against itself shall not stand."

From these biblical passages Abraham Lincoln, at the Republican Convention in Springfield, on June 16, 1858, presented his now-famous "House Divided" speech in an attempt to persuade the Illinois Legislature to elect him to the United States Senate (for that's how it was done in those days). Despite its powerful resonance with historians, the Illinois Legislature chose, instead, Lincoln's chief antagonist and oratorical opponent, Stephen A. Douglas. Did the politicians know too much of Lincoln's character to prefer Douglas? Does that old saying "familiarity breeds contempt" apply here?

This speech was hailed as a remarkable and memorable statement describing the continuing state of friction between the North and South. What historians have failed to point out was that besides this perceptive analysis, Lincoln reveals (as in many of his later ones) a firmness and resolution of uncompromising rigidity that, in the hands of a powerful leader, might be characterized as tyrannical and dictatorial. Observe the firmness, "I believe this government cannot endure permanently half slave and half free. I do not expect the Union to be dissolved; I do not expect the house to fall; but I do expect that it will cease to be divided. It will become all one thing or all the other." Sometime later, looking into his crystal ball and commenting upon the friction, he prophesied the Civil War. "In my opinion it will not cease until a crisis should have been reached and passed."

LINCOLN AND "BAD BARGAIN"

Throughout his whole life, Lincoln remembered and followed one of his father's favorite sayings, "If you make a bad bargain, hug it all the tighter." This fatalistic outlook seemed to be a guiding principle and profound influence upon Lincoln in his manner of solving problems. Here it should be pointed out that, when the thirteen colonies merged themselves into the United States, they were, in reality, two countries, North and South, with distinct political, economic, and social structures so dissimilar as to be ultimately antagonistic to each other's interests. It was the industrial, aggressive, clever North versus the largely agrarian slave-based, aristocratic South. The Union was, therefore, a "bad bargain" thrust together for their mutual benefit in opposing the mother country, Britain, and without this togetherness the enterprise would have failed. Despite the gigantic differences of these "two nations," it was Lincoln's motivating obsession and determination to "hug it all the tighter." He would brutally suppress the South's attempt at self-determination to keep them in the Union even if he had to kill every one of them to do so. Thus, ironically, he proved the biblical logic "every kingdom divided against itself is brought to desolation; and every city or house divided against itself shall not stand."

How is it that such a basically irreligious man as Abraham Lincoln so often used biblical allusions in his speeches, arguments and debates? As a clever lawyer, and he was most certainly that, he would use every and any tactic to win his case and the Bible proved to be a major reference book. Knowing that America was a deeply religious nation, and the people quite familiar with biblical teachings, Lincoln's allusions resonated favorably within the community. On numerous occasions, either judicial, political, or just plain oratorical, conclusions or verdicts favorable to Lincoln usually resulted if biblical references were used.

An additional skill, which should not be overlooked in Lincoln's armamentarium, is his remarkable ability to simplify the issues to be considered to distill them down to their very essences and present them to the public in a clear concise manner. Time and again his productions sparkle and shine with these characteristics. None shines more brightly in all its glory than the world famous Gettysburg Address, a document of only 271 words and not one of them unnecessary!

DICTATOR

If we define a dictator as one who uses violence, repression, and ethnic cleansing as political tools then Abraham Lincoln certainly deserves that epithet. Although America was originally settled by the same type of people, primarily Anglo-Saxon, there evolved two distinct classes of people in two separate parts of the country, North and South. The South was characterized as agrarian and aristocratic in manners, whereas the North evolved as an industrial, capitalistic society. The dictionary defines "ethnic" as "of or relating to races or large groups of people classed according to common traits and customs" my conclusion is that "ethnic cleansing" is appropriate in describing the political, economic and military altercations that was known as the American Civil War!

No matter how egregious the "sins" of the South are portrayed by the politicians, historians and abolitionists, they did not merit the harsh and arrant treatment as they were obliged to endure. The unbridled butchery and devastation by Lincoln, and his minions was an unconscionable overresponse and a stain upon the honor of a supposed Christian nation. They responded as a self-righteous angel, following in the footsteps of the lunatic John Brown, destroying and devastating everything and everyone in its path.

LINCOLN DICTATORSHIP

Considering Lincoln had no executive experience prior to becoming the chief executive of one of the most powerful nations of the world, he took over with a breathless rapacity seldom seen prior to or subsequent to his administration. By delaying a special calling of Congress on July 4, 1861, he had eleven weeks from the firing on Fort Sumter on March 5, 1861, to exert virtual dictatorial powers to crush the rebellion without the constitutionally required guidance of the Congress, i.e., the legislative branch. During this time he had unprecedented executive authority. Cleverly hiding behind the first few words of article II and invoking "war powers" necessity he intruded on military, legislative, executive, and some judicial powers, actions of questionable constitutional character.

On April 15, he called out "the militia of several states of the Union, to the aggregate number of seventy five thousand" in order to suppress the rebellion and enforce the laws.

On April 19, he ordered the blockade of the ports of the seceded states.

On April 20, he enlarged the navy by nineteen vessels.

On April 20, he proceeded to take a number of extraordinary steps by himself, again without legislative interference. First, he closed the post office to "treasonable correspondence." Second, he had arrested people "being or about to engage in disloyal and treasonable practices" by special civil and military agencies and detained in military custody. Third, he obtained a temporary loan of 1/4 billion dollars.

On April 27, he empowers the commanding general of the Army to suspend the writ of habeas corpus(a distinct constitutional prerogative of Congress).

On May 3, he calls for volunteers for three years.

Of course, being a clever and careful lawyer, he had a plausible explanation for his actions: "It became necessary for me to choose whether, using only the existing means, agencies and processes which Congress had provided, I should let the government fall at once into ruin or whether, availing myself of the broader powers conferred by the Constitution in cases of insurrection, I would make an effort to save if, with all its blessings, for the present age and for posterity." For his actions of a more legislative and, therefore, constitutionally more doubtful character, he gave a different justification: "These measures, whether strictly legal or not, were ventured upon, under what appeared to be a popular demand, and a public necessity; trusting then, as now, that Congress would readily ratify them. It is believed that nothing has been done beyond the Constitutional competency of Congress."(Note, there seems to be a deliberate deflection with considering the Constitutional competency of himself in these matters.) The Great Oz has spoken and he does not want anyone to question him on his questionable actions. "Let us move on" is his fervent desire.

His line of reasoning is that in times of urgent necessity or emergency (as in war!) an official of a constitutional state may act more faithfully to his oath of office if he breaks one or two laws in order to preserve all the others. On the basis of "war power" necessity he took the heady route of power politics taking one extraordinary action after another to justify his behavior. He considered himself therefore, constitutionally empowered to do just about anything that the military situation demanded. He is quoted as saying, "As Commander in Chief in time of war, I suppose I have a right to take any measure which may best subdue the enemy." He, thus, honored the spirit of the Constitution by stretching the letter almost to its limits.

One might compare the life of Lincoln with other subsequent dictators—Hitler, Stalin, Mao, Pol Pot—all leaders whose narrow focus led them on paths of cold-blooded butchery to achieve those goals.

Seemingly, Lincoln did not believe in or denied the sovereignty of the people.

In discussing the recognition of the Confederacy in the British parliament many were antagonized by Lincoln's suspension of habeas corpus, the imprisonment of political dissent and the North's restrictions of freedom of the press.

Using military tribunals Lincoln obviated the use of civilian courts which gave defendants, through long-established principles, certain well-defined rights including trial by jury. If gives the defendant a degree of fairness and fairness is considered the "American Way." Military courts are not designed to give defendants the same rights and protections as in civilian courts. During the Civil War. Five thousand military tribunals were convened to handle somewhere between 14,000 and 15,000 defendants. As there did not arise any outcry regarding due process and fairness, Lincoln had a free hand in dealing with those charged with the power of a virtual dictator!

Many years ago Machiavelli concluded that all republics required the leadership along the lines of a dictator who, in times of stress (cases of extreme exigency) could respond quickly to events without being constrained by such impediments as the rules and regulations of a Constitutional document and be able to assume absolute power in the form of temporary dictatorship. On pages 58 and 59 in his book, *The Imperial Presidency*, Arthur M. Schlesinger Jr. describes how Abraham Lincoln had, as Benjamin R. Curtis described, "a military despotism.""He wielded more authority than any single Englishman has done since Oliver Cromwell." Schlesinger goes on, "Since Lincoln's reputation as the greatest of democratic statesmen is well earned, he obviously did not become a despot lightly. He was like Cromwell, the Protector. The nation, as he saw it, faced the most desperate of emergencies. Its very survival was at stake. (To me this is a preposterous assertion, for both halves had the inherent capabilities of surviving and prospering independently) and with it the survival of 'free government upon the earth' should they go their own way."

Using military tribunals Lincoln obviated the use of civilian courts, which gave defendants, through long-established principles, certain well-defined rights including trial by jury. It gives the defendant a degree of fairness and fairness is considered the "American way". Military courts are not designed to give defendants the same rights and protections as in civilian courts. During the Civil War, 5,000 military tribunals were convened to handle somewhere between 14,000 and 15,000 defendants. As there did not arise any outcry regarding due process and fairness, Lincoln had a free hand in dealing with those charged with the power of a virtual dictator!

During the war years Edwin Stanton had caused the arrest of 38,000 persons with even the flimsiest of evidence of any wrong doing. With the suspension of habeas corpus this task was made so easy as to be preposterous as the large numbers indicate.

[In discussing the recognition of the Confederacy in the British parliament many were antagonized by Lincoln's suspension of habeas corpus, the imprisonment of political dissenter and the North's restrictions of freedom of the press, out even these considerations were insufficient move them to support the South.] Or was it more retribution upon their upstart lost brethren?

LINCOLN DICTATOR

In the History Today magazine of February 2010, Frank Prochaska, who teaches history at Yale University, presents some viewpoints of the English political journalist, Walter Bagehot who wrote over thirty articles on America in the 1860s. Though highly critical of the American Constitution, and how inflexible it was, he also has some backhanded comments on Abraham Lincoln, where he credits him with "saving the Union." Mr. Prochaska goes on to say: "In Lincoln, Bagehot found his ideal American ruler, an enlightened despot whose 'dictatorship' was excused by the extreme circumstances of the day." I too agree that Lincoln acted as a dictator, but I am infuriated by how so many historians have swallowed the bullshit that Lincoln's actions amounted to justifiable homicide, and how casually they accept the deaths of over 600,000Americans in this unnecessary and preventable confrontation! It was sheer madness with barbaric lunatics of the Hatfield/McCoy hillbillies' types fighting to the death where calm negotiations should have prevented it all! The British, under the guidance, hectoring, and pestering of William Wilberforce solved the thorny issue of slavery with minimal effusion of blood. Were the Americans so defective in capacity to do as well? It was because the enlightened despot, Abraham Lincoln, was incapable of compromise, of negotiation, of give and take to arrive at a sensible conclusion. With vehemence and an unbending will he imposed a gory solution upon a prostrate South. Despite his seemingly mild exterior, he was the picture-perfect school-yard bully.

DICTATOR LINCOLN

Much as constitutional government ceased to exist once Caesar, Crassus, and Pompey formed the first Roman triumvirate, so too did it cease to exist once Lincoln's cabinet was formed, especially with Edwin Stanton, Salmon Chase, and William Seward. Citing emergency powers granted to the president in times of war Lincoln acted as a virtual dictator!

Taking their cue from the bombastic bullshit utterance of Edwin Stanton, "Now he belongs to the ages," the American historian has carried on the tradition of hood-winking the American public, much as a perpetual motion machine, churning out sycophantic book after book after book, account after account after account, continuing the idolatrous worship of a bull in a china shop!

Apparently, Abraham Lincoln did not learn the principal lesson from the Declaration of Independence. Where it said "all men are created equal" Lincoln determined that the people of the South were less equal than those of the North in his blind and merciless crushing of the South, all for the character flaw of exploiting a backward, primitive people!

DICTATOR

If we could gather together a large group of historians (prominent), but only those with unbiased outlook and critical views, then I am most confident they would add, as I would, Abraham Lincoln to the list of the world's cruelest dictators. To accomplish this feat they would have to avoid and ignore all the bullshit and propaganda that has been rammed down our throats ever since Edwin M. Stanton uttered. "Now he belongs to the ages." Only a dictator of monomaniacal bent could impose his forceful will upon a pliant population, goading them into killing their follow men in the pursuit of some nebulous utopian goal of universal brotherhood to the tune of over 1,000,000 poor souls dumped by the tons in gargantuan cemeteries.

Although Lincoln apologists have succeeded in portraying him as the benign, avuncular Abraham, events during the American Civil War clearly prove otherwise. Only a man of steely resolve and firm determination would have pressed the nation to embark on such a bloody and brutal pursuit of submission of the South in what we might call the American Holocaust. By doing so he revealed the attributes and mentality of the totalitarian, a brutal unyielding butcher who thought nothing of wasting 1,000,000 Americans (North and South) in pursuit of freeing 4,000,000 slaves. Any man who could do this is not a man of delicate sensibilities, but moreover a fiendish brute who should *not* be placed in the pantheon of heroes but of that of such hateful luminaries as Genghis Khan, Hitler, Stalin, Pol Pot, etc.

DEVIOUS LINCOLN

The fundamental fact that should always kept in mind, despite the success Lincoln backers have achieved in portraying him as saintly, is that Lincoln was an attorney and a politician! These two facts, by themselves, should automatically disqualify him from consideration of secular sainthood. He was a clever, devious, and manipulative person and these skills brought him great success as an attorney, a debater, and finally a politician. To distract the nation's attention from the reality that the Civil War was in truth fought over the issue of slavery he would always insist that it was a noble crusade to "preserve the Union." In his first inaugural address he mentions the "Union" twenty times. In his first message to Congress on July 4, 1861, he used the word "Union" thirty-two times. I view this as a clever way of focusing the nation's attention on his agenda. Years later Joseph Goebbels, Hitler's propaganda minister, would adopt this technique of repeating a lie often enough that it acquired a semblance of truth to the general, unquestioning minds.

Thus, the reality that the war was truly a conflict between the Yankee capitalist bourgeoisie and the aristocratic planter class, and the advantage of slave labor over wage labor was cleverly obfuscated. Once Lincoln determined that he was dealing with forces or "combinations too powerful to be suppressed by the ordinary course of judicial proceedings" he resorted to man's primitive nature, of bloody conquest, to achieve his political objectives! In the realm of world philosophy Lincoln had a narrow, constricted outlook reflecting his parochial upbringing more typical of a backwoods, barroom brawler than a contemplative deep thinker.

BUTCHER

If we accept the long-held premise that the institution of slavery is incompatible with the individualist and libertarian values common to dissenting Protestantism and politics at thought of the Enlightenment then the logical question must inescapably follow, "How do we convince our Southern brethren that the long-held habit of the exploitation of man by man… of one man 'owning' another man in perpetual bondage is wrongful and unacceptable by today's standards." Many words by many people were exchanged by both sides on this thorny issue as the South, ever resentful of the attacks upon their "peculiar institution" refuse to accept the North's position.

However, just as Alexander the Great solved the very complex problem of the Gordian knot by taking out his sword and unraveling the knot by cutting it, so too did Abraham Lincoln solve the equally complicated issue of slavery in the South by taking out his sword and with the torch laid waste the South. None but a cold-blooded butcher could push his own people into the jaws of death and over the cliff and into the abyss. None but a callous son-of-a-bitch could then shed crocodile tears reading the casualty lists, of the tragic loss of so many "brave young men" when he himself had the ultimate power to stop the insanity, to stop the carnage, to stop the unnecessary effusion of blood! No wonder he seemed so depressed on so many occasions! Upon reading these lists only a man totally devoid of conscience would fail to be moved to tears of guilt and remorse.

Even granting the "unimaginable horrors" of slavery, the most significant question we must answer: is the evil of slavery worse than the slaughter of over 620,000 Americans, the devastation and ruin of cities North and South, with the enormous cost included? To win a minor victory of emancipation did Lincoln have to trash America to achieve the abolitionists' vision? This seems to me a grotesquely distorted sense of values

In 1858, in one of his famous debates with Stephen Douglas, Lincoln predicted, after affirming the total wrongness of slavery that "I do not suppose that in the most peaceful way ultimate extinction would occur in less than 100 years at the least." Instead of a long, arduous, but peaceful road to emancipation impatient Lincoln preferred the sword and gunpowder for more immediate resolution. The loss of so many lives seemed of minor significance and consequence, a mere bump in the road to freedom for the slaves!

BRUTISH LINCOLN

Certain writers other than myself have uttered unflattering comments regarding the reign of Abraham Lincoln. In the Atlantic Monthly, April 2002, Mr. Christopher Hitchens states, "But one might as readily have summarized Lincoln's hesitations and evasions on the matter of slavery and abolition, and his long and tortuous attempts to avoid war, and his preference for the survival of the Union over other questions of principle. Yet when the arrogant exorbitance of 'the Slave Power' compelled a confrontation, there was no length to which Lincoln would not go; no abolitionist group, however fanatical, that he would not befriend; and no extremity of pitiless violence to which he would not resort. His gift—better to say his instinct—for unifying and spirited phrasing promoted him well above the sordid battlefields for which those phrases were carpentered." I have always regarded Mr. Hitchens as a remarkable, unbiased, and trenchant observer of the world scene, and time and again have enjoyed his incisive observations. His British upbringing seems to have insulated him from and left him unpolluted by the propagandist literature of the Lincoln Adulation Industry for which I am forever grateful.

GETTYSBURG, THE MISSED OPPORTUNITY

Upon reading several accounts surrounding the battle of Gettysburg, I can only imagine the fury of Abraham Lincoln at his generals for missing another golden opportunity. Instead of licking their wounds and attending to the dying he, seemingly alone, recognized that they should have pursued the defeated and demoralized Confederate forces before they could cross the Potomac River to the safety of Virginia. They would have capped their victory by the total annihilation of the retreating forces. He may have been an armchair general, but he was endowed with the features of a backwoods, barroom brawler with tenacity and determination to be the last man standing. It was a colossal blunder, an opportunity to shorten the war. Again Lincoln had to deal with timid generals, a plague that dogged him from the outset of hostilities. It is precisely this type of situation Lincoln was referring to when confronted with the reported drinking problem of Grant. His reply was for the complaint to discover Grant's brand of whiskey so that he could order it for his other generals.

Lincoln said he could not spare the man. "He fights!"

IMPATIENT LINCOLN
SLAVERY—HISTORICAL OVERVIEW

The "first emancipation of Negro slaves," the beginning of a movement against the slave trade and against slavery, began in the last quarter of the eighteenth century. Vermont started it in 1777, New York in 1827, and a progressive cascade followed until the decision of all the states north of the Mason-Dixon line to end slavery within their borders. Pressure from humanitarian-based antislavery societies contributed to the progression in thinking and acting to restrict slavery in these states and then declaring total abolition. By 1792, every state from Massachusetts to Virginia had an active manumission and antislavery society. Particularly in New York, which had a slave population larger than all the Northern states combined, numbering 21,000, male white workers exerted political pressure to emancipate the slaves. This was because they were unwilling or incapable of competing with slave labor.

During this time a significant number of Negroes had achieved emancipation and were designated as "free." They owed their status to several reasons, they purchased their own release; others, usually relatives, purchased their release; they secured their release for good service; or they were born of nonslave mothers. An interesting fact, that should be pointed out is that, throughout the slavery period that ended in 1865, more "free" blacks lived in the South than in the North.

Another little known fact is that, based on a proclamation by British General Dunmore during the American Revolution, many slaves offered to join the British army in exchange for their freedom. Not to be outdone, the rebellious colonies offered blacks liberty in exchange for military service. By all accounts, as many as 5,000 former slaves fought for the colonies, and thousands more fought for the British. An additional large number also "obtained freedom by running away from their places of enslavement during the unsettled time of warfare, estimates running as high as 20%

As slavery was an international activity, and that no international laws were ever passed outlawing it, many considered that the force used to suppress the slave trade in reality violated international law! This did not seem to bother the do-gooders in the least!

Blinded by their zealotry, made drunk by their compassion for the downtrodden slave, determined that their view should prevail, they charged blindly ahead to demand the liberation of the slaves.

Years of Definitive Abolition of Slavery
Slavery Ended by Conflict
St. Domingue, 1793
United States, 1863
Slavery Ended by European Power
British Caribbean, 1838
French Caribbean, 1848
Danish Caribbean, 1848
Dutch Caribbean, 1863
Puerto Rico, 1873
Cuba, 1886
Slavery Ended after Independence
Chile, 1823
Central America, 1824
Mexico, 1829
Slavery Ended by Law
Colombia, 1851
Ecuador, 1852
Argentina, 1853
Uruguay, 1853
Peru, 1854
Venezuela, 1854
Bolivia, 1861
Paraguay, 1869
Brazil, 1888

Out of five European powers, ten South American countries, Central America, and Mexico, only two involved violent and bloody conflict to resolve the issue of slavery. To its eternal shame, one of these was the United States; the other St. Domingue (Haiti), a backward society. Thus, we have nineteen civilian societies who managed to "solve" the "problem" of slavery by peaceful, enlightened cerebrations and only one that could not control its bloodthirsty lust and passion for immediate resolution. Led by a clever lawyer/politician with an inflexible will of iron, and power to do so, led the lemminglike country hurtling into the abyss of blood, gore, and carnage, and yet, by the action of devious bullshitter "historians," emerged with the patina of knights heroic acting in a crusade of the highest moral dimensions!

The greatest error of the politicians of that day, and the historians, was the failure to take into account the "big picture" or "worldview." The inexorable world opinion and action was against slavery, and it was only a matter of time when that institution was no more. But that required patience, a feature lacking in the make-up of Abraham Lincoln!

LINCOLN THE MAN

GREATNESS OF LINCOLN?

As the many speeches and debates of Abraham Lincoln are read reread and studied, and even today quoted by memory by his many admirers, it becomes apparent and obvious that his greatness lay as a speech writer and debater. With his training as a lawyer he carefully prepared his "cases" with a step-by-step reasoned and well-structured argument, clarity as opposed to other writer's obfuscation, brevity instead of garrulousness, leading his hearers toward his point of view. He spent many long hours laboring over his presentations, writing and rewriting searching for *le mot juste* or *l'idée correcte* until he achieved the exact effect to persuade the audience to his point view. With this almost magical power to persuade the nation of the righteousness of his cause, Lincoln became a virtual Pied Piper leading America along his path to a virtual utopia here on earth. Unfortunately, he was more than a heard of lemmings leading the nation over a cliff to their doom in the catastrophe of the Civil War! Therefore, in my humble estimation, he was an unmitigated disaster!

Under his presidency more lives were lost in this short four year period than in *all* the battles in which this great nation participated, combined! The dreadful loss of over 600,000 America, North and South, exceeds the losses in all other wars—the Revolutionary War, the War with Mexico, the Spanish-American War, WW I, WW II, Korea, Vietnam, etc. Contrary to the opinion of others, I view him as a loose cannon, ready to plunge this nation into a bloody confrontation, never patient to negotiate and compromise. The situation required the difficult task of negotiation rather than the easy brainless approach of the iron-fisted, virtual dictatorship of Abraham Lincoln. In his monomaniacal pursuit of forced Union, an unnatural integration of two very dissimilar societies, he would rather pursue a course of undreamed of brutality than work for a peaceful, bloodless solution.

LINCOLN'S FAME AND REPUTATION

Abraham Lincoln is remembered primarily for his role in leading the North in the Civil War and the emancipation of the slaves, but in my opinion he should be remembered more for his literary and oratorical skills. As a reflection of his legal background and training to be a lawyer, his writings, orations and debates take on the appearance of a well-constructed legal document. They are remembered for their lofty, profound and lasting utterances, with clear simple phrasing, showing the logical progression of an attorney's mind and, as Ken Burns said, he had "an almost mystical ability to get to get to the heart of things." Much as a plodding bricklayer he first established a firm foundation, then slowly and methodically built his case brick by brick until he completed a strong legal edifice. By using the well-known nowadays KISS (keep it simple, stupid) principle and keenly aware of his audiences' lack of sophistication he managed to persuade many listeners to his side of the argument, whether it be jury, listeners to his debates or lastly, the voting public.

But a man is more than the words that flow from his mouth. He must also be judged by his actions, and, by judging Abraham Lincoln thusly. I am of the opinion that he was an unmitigated disaster. Despite his characterization as a compassionate man, there seemed to be not an ounce of compromise in him. Upon achieving the presidency, he seemed to be drunk with the power of that office, ruling as a virtual dictator, imposing his inflexible will upon his cabinet and, therefore, the nation. The Civil War was characterized as a string of butcheries each equally, or more, horrendous than the previous one. With unwavering and unrelenting vehemence he pursued this slaughter policy until almost all the draft-age men were killed.

Rather than the Lincoln Memorial tribute to the man, where his words, thoughts, and ideas are represented, a more fitting monument, one that reflects the horrific number of dead soldiers wasted, in my opinion, should be erected instead. I recommend the casting of over 1,000,000 bronze statues all in different poses of agony of dead and dying and piling them up in a great mound next to and probably dwarfing the Washington monument. This presentation would be a stunning, eye-popping gruesomeness of carnage, bringing home the stark reality of the wasteful, tragic expenditure of so many lives for so little purpose. Hopefully, even at this late juncture, it might arouse more tears and sadness than the Vietnam memorial for the losses there were a mere 50,000, a pittance in comparison to the 1,000,000 Civil War dead.

An historian, Richard Carwardine, praised him as "a political leader so thoughtful in his use of language, so careful in his preparation of speeches." To me this is what should be considered as the crowning achievement of Lincoln. As a political leader he was a monumental disaster plunging the nation into a war that was totally unnecessary, a war that should have been averted by compromise and negotiation, not by endless bloody war.

LINCOLN'S CHARACTER

As an avid reader Abraham Lincoln was very much caught up in the philosophical currents of his time and became fervently idealistic upon reading those articulated in both the Declaration of Independence and the Constitution. Embracing these idealisms with a passion "that all men are created equal… that they are endowed by their Creator with certain inalienable rights… that among these are life, liberty, and the pursuit of happiness" (property), he then felt compelled to bestow these rights upon even the lowliest of low—the slaves. It became paramount in Lincoln's mind, impatient and obsessed, to immediately rectify this serious omission, not at some vague future date, not tomorrow, but immediately! Compromise and negotiation were not in his nature, unless it was from a position of dominance and superior power. Drunk with the power of the presidency, he proceeded to propel the nation headlong into the bloodiest mutual slaughter that ever occurred on American soil!

Herndon, one of the guardians of his memory, described Lincoln thusly, "uprightness, integrity, cordiality and kindness of heart, amenity of manner, and his strict attention not only to the rights but to the feelings of all." But of all the accolades that are heaped upon the head of Abraham Lincoln, none is more bizarre, none is more grotesque than to characterize him as the "nation's savior" or "the redeemer president." Grotesque because of the implied parallel to the death of Jesus Christ upon the cross! And that was to redeem the sins of the world! Any attempt to equate Lincoln's life with that of Jesus Christ would be sheer blasphemy.

LINCOLN'S CHARACTER

Year after year as historians run out of encomiums concerning Abraham Lincoln, they stretch and strain to add greater and greater superlatives till at last their utterances become so bizarre as to be laughable. Initially, they gave us that bullshit that might appeal to simple minds, i.e., he was the quintessential "common man," the "rail splitter" and "Honest Abe" ad nauseam. Later someone called him Machiavellian for they saw in him a clever political deviousness. They then challenged our credulity by comparing him to Jesus Christ for, in "preserving the Union," he could justifiably be called "savior" of his country. Even though it is common to regard rulers and leaders of one's country with such an appellation, I have difficulty with such an assertion.

To save the world and mankind it was Jesus Christ himself who suffered and died upon the cross. It was his blood that was spilled. It was he who bore the agony. It was he who made the ultimate sacrifice. Abraham Lincoln, however, in prosecuting the bloodiest war in American history to the fullest, shed the blood of the American soldiers, North and South, brothers, upon the battlefields. It is they who made the ultimate sacrifice. Not he! It is they who deserve the name "saviors of America."

It has been said that because of the national trespass of slavery that shaped his presidency, we can readily think of him as "wounded for our transgressions" and "bruised for our iniquities." Some portray him as a suffering servant doing what he had to do to save the Union, and a man of sorrows and acquainted with grief when reading the casualty lists but not sufficiently moved out of his torpor to stop the insanity.

Others attempt to compliment him by saying he was calculating and inexorable in his acceptance of the enormous casualties incurred. This is no compliment! In my mind he was a bloody butcher, unrelenting in imposing his will through the power of the presidential office, crushing the South and wrecking the country in the process. To likewise describe him as a man of simple and exceptional goodness flies in the face of facts. Over 600,000 Americans perished in this fiasco.

Yet to my astonishment no one and I mean no one has questioned the facts or has been critical of the events and personalities involved in pushing forward this dispute to such a calamitous conclusion. No court of enquiry, no commission, no panel of experts, no study was ever made to determine if a different conclusion could have been achieved, i.e., without such a horrendous lose in lives. All the historians act as if they had been paid off by the abolitionists, to keep silent, to focus our attention on the positive aspects of the dispute, i.e., the Union had been saved, as if this were the Holy Grail. The rebels were portrayed as worse than the Huns, more evil than Nazis, more treacherous than Communists, in essence the greatest evil that could have befallen mankind and, therefore, deserved to die. I find this casual attitude astonishing.

As the casualty reports were published in all the newspapers the general populace was stunned into silence, to the quiet submission and acceptance without objection or complaint, with a fatalism that boggles the mind. No voices could be found to say "Stop this insanity! Much as the backward hillbillies Hatfields and McCoys carried on a bloody family feud over the minor incident of a theft of a pig, so too did the North and South slaughter each other with a vehemence that is unheard of. Peaceful resolution, compromise, negotiation were not words in their lexicon. Brute force was!

An example of Lincoln's brutality occurred after the Sioux uprising in 1862 that killed hundreds of settlers, Lincoln approved one of the largest executions in U.S. military history, the hanging of thirty-eight Indians. The total history of Abraham Lincoln was elaborately constructed to portray him as a secular saint. Hundreds of historians followed this clever deception.

Perhaps John Maynard Keynes was referring to leaders such as Lincoln when he wrote "Madmen in authority, who hear voices in the air, are usually distilling their frenzy from some academic scribbler of a few years back."

CHARACTER

The acolytes and kiss-ass sycophantic historians of Abraham Lincoln, in order to maintain his noble image, characterize his rule as "one of America's greatest presidents" because "he provided strong leadership, set a clear course and articulated a moral vision to guide the nation through difficult times." Through all the verbiage they have carefully obscured the fact that one million Americans were sacrificed to emancipate four million slaves, such a ghastly number that it should, in ordinary circumstances, qualify Lincoln to the pantheon of megalomaniacal butchers of all time! Similar to Goebbels and Hitler, they have repeated and continue to repeat the lies so incessantly as to give an appearance of veracity concerning the man. The created myth is now settled dogma that has developed a cult following of historian automatons and zombies with no evidence of cerebral activity!

THE CHARACTER OF LINCOLN

History often instructs us that in situations of adversity man have the remarkable capacity to often rise to the occasion and deal effectively with the situation. The events leading up to the American Civil War required a man of great tact and remarkable diplomacy in dealing with the thorny issues confronting the political class in dealing with the controversial problem of slavery. Abraham Lincoln was not that man. In his very soul, and apart and distinct from his empathetic exterior, he was a rigid, stubborn, unyielding lawyer/politician whose true nature resembled that of a ham-fisted, backwoods, barroom brawler who, when angered, could exhibit a ruthlessness of unparalleled ferocity. Witness the deaths of over 1,000,000 American young men wasted over the problem of slavery, an issue that should have been solved, like in many other nations, with bloodless diplomacy! Lincoln had the negotiating skills of an Adolf Hitler, Joseph Stalin, and a whole host of other brutal dictators who characteristically solved their problems by the application of a crushing mailed fist! For a man who is portrayed as a loving father figure he was most certainly capable of acts of monstrous destruction!

CHARACTER

The Library of Congress counts 4,925 books written on Abraham Lincoln, second only to the number of books written on the Bible, and both continue to grow daily. The sad, but true, fact is that these 4,925 books, in their ovine obsession to emulate, and perhaps outdo those who have written before, have only added to the bullshit life of Abraham Lincoln. They repeatedly offer his portraiture as a saintly but firm God-like savior of the nation when it was threatened with disintegration. But they carefully avoid also the God-like portraiture of a wrathful, vengeful tyrant who prosecuted a bloody war without surcease. They maintain that only a man with exemplary characteristics could have "saved the nation" from the ruination as Southern secession would surely have had. Bullshit! Bullshit! He was a monomaniacal butcher devoid of any talent to apply himself to the difficult task of calm, patient, protracted and laborious negotiations to achieve a mutually satisfactory solution. It required compromise. It required arbitration. It required give and take. This was not in his DNA. Tyranny was!

WHAT PRICE?

As one of the characters of George Bernard Shaw's Major Barbara asked, "What price, salvation?" I ask, "What price, emancipation?" "What price, secession?" Over one million American souls were trashed so that four million slaves could go free. Was this price justified? None in the 4,925 books deigned to ask this delicate question. To these historians, as well as the instigators of the War, it was justifiable homicide in pursuit of a noble cause and salutary purpose. Bullshit, say I again! It was murder! Most foul! It was slaughter! It was genocide! It was ethnic cleansing! It was all of the above!

JUSTIFICATION OF LINCOLN'S ACTIONS

In 1990, in an article on "Man of the Millennium," George Will justifies Abraham Lincoln as a candidate for man of the millennium by stating: "Lincoln, by winning, as only he could have done, the Civil War, (Does he mean by the unparalleled butchery?) prevented the proliferation of petty, unlovely little nations in what is now the United States. He prevented the victory of, among other bad things, the idea of secession. The idea would have caused the disintegration of even the Confederacy, and perhaps what remained of the Union, too."

I am amazed at the clarity of Mr. Will's crystal ball and the certainty he displays in prognosticating what would happen should the South be allowed to secede. To forestall such an eventuality did Lincoln have to butcher so many Americans to achieve his goal? I am in total disagreement that such a fateful outcome would have eventuated. In my opinion the two halves would have gone their own way, surviving quite well, bound by ties of common ancestry independent yet cooperative with each other in matters of mutual interest. Their respective societies would achieve certain stability with a worldview compatible with the outlooks of their respective societies much as what Canada and America now enjoy!

Mr. Will seems to forget that Jefferson's formulation that "governments derive their just powers from the consent of the governed" comes from the profound philosophical pronouncements of John Locke. Mr. Will should also remember that Mr. Locke went on to elucidate his treatise by saying to the effect, that if government proves destructive of their duty to adequately protect its citizens or abuses them in any way, it is the *retained right of the citizens* to abolish that government and to form one that is more suitable to their likings. Ergo, the legitimacy of the South to secede from the abusive Union that Will so worships.

LINCOLN'S SKILLS AS AN ATTORNEY

In May 1850, a newspaper, the Danville "Illinois Citizen," published this assessment of Abraham Lincoln's skills as an attorney. It began, "rough, uncouth and unattractive, stern... slow and guarded," yet "profound in the depths of his musings... He lives to ponder, reflect and cogitate... in his examination of witnesses, he displays a masterly ingenuity... that baffles concealment and defies deceit. And in addressing a jury, there is no false glitter, no sickly sentimentalism to be discovered. In vain we look for a rhetorical display... Seizing upon the minutest points, he weaves them into his argument with an ingenuity really astonishing. Bold, forcible and energetic, he forces conviction upon the mind, and, by his clearness and conciseness, stamps it there, not to be erased... Such are some of the qualities that place Mr. L. at the head of the profession in this State."

Whether it be through the many legal cases Lincoln argued in court, or the various debates in which he participated, or the many addresses and speeches he gave, it becomes very apparent that he excelled in what Aristotle, 2,400 years ago, called "rhetoric." By this I mean he expressed himself precisely and clearly, formulating an argumentative thesis à la Aristotle, specifically targeting his audience to persuade them to his point of view. Time after time, case after case, speech after speech, debate after debate all reveal to the world how carefully he crafted and prepared his rhetoric, becoming a master in its use, all so memorable as to remain monuments and testaments to his virtuosity!

These observations by qualified and dispassionate people, that Lincoln's skills lay primarily for lawyering and debating and, when he showed this ability in the Lincoln-Douglas debates, the masses misinterpreted these talents as eminently suitable for leading the nation as president of the United States. In my humble opinion he was miscast in this role where tact and diplomacy, give and take and, above all, compromise are essential for successful negotiations. Instead, once propelled into the highest office in the land by self-serving, behind-the-scenes powerbrokers, he revealed his gross ineptitude for the job. His rigidity and megalomania compelled him to embark on a mission to slaughter so many young Americans for such a trivial cause as the issue of slavery, and never once pausing to reconsider his views that were leading to the destruction of the nation.

Compromise was not in his nature. Imposition of his iron will upon the nation was, and the gravestones of over 1,000,000 young Americans are, a testament to the tragedy of his presidency!

HYPOCRISY

Even though New England had close ties with the mother country, economic, cultural, and genetic, these facts did not prevent them from striving for control of their own destiny—freedom from the virtually dictatorial control of a dominating partner. However, what they objected to in their British parent, i.e., the tendency to dominate and dictate to an obstreperous offspring, they borrowed and applied to the South without stopping to consider neither the inconsistency, the irony nor the hypocrisy of that behavior. Hiding behind the facade of moral indignation over the issue of slavery, they showed their British bloody brutality and arbitrariness of Old England by first giving them a nonnegotiable demand for release of the slaves, and when this was not acceded to, crushing them mercilessly.

Of course this demand could not be met! Having been addicted to slavery for over two hundred years, this demand was a dagger aimed at the heart of the South's economy; going "cold turkey" would surely end in economic disruption, chaos and eventually disaster. As such it had to be rejected categorically. The South had to fight for its freedom once again. This alone, with its colleagues of similar interests, but from a more determined, richer, more powerful, more malignant, but unfortunately more proximate oppressor than Britain. Their attitude of "your economy be damned, your welfare be damned, your freedom be damned; we have decided your fate. Do it!"

The South attempted to articulate forms of natural-rights doctrine in political theory. Ideas of self-determination were enunciated but totally ignored by the North. Liberty and property, the twin "household gods of Englishmen" were ideas now considered alien in America and suppressed by the philistine North.

HYPOCRISY(?) OF LINCOLN

John A. Logan of Illinois felt confident that Lincoln would go slow in starting a Civil War, having been "so conscientious about the Mexican war as to oppose it." Stephen Douglas echoed this sentiment when he said, "that Mr. Lincoln, after having emerged from the surroundings of a small country village… will sink the partisan in the patriot… by repudiating his extreme doctrines of a party" (Sandburg).

The compassion that he showed toward the Mexican nation in his speech before Congress in 1848 was nowhere to be found in regards to his fellow Americans of the South when they too voiced their natural rights of self-determination. This right was reserved to a foreign nation in 1848 but viciously denied to his fellow countrymen. How can this inconsistency be explained, this unbridled magnanimity for the Mexicans, but unbridled rigidity and brutality for his own people? Am I the only one who sees hypocrisy, or did his about face in twelve years represent miraculous epiphany?

Abraham Lincoln's speech before Congress in 1848 reveals a man strongly influenced by John Locke's philosophy that seemed to have faded and disappeared from his consciousness over a few years. He said, "Any people anywhere being inclined and having the power have the right to rise up and shake off the existing government, and form a new one that suits them better. This is a most valuable, a most sacred right-a right which we hope and believe is to liberate the world. Nor is this right confined to cases in which the whole people of an existing government may choose to exercise it. *Any portion of such people that can* may revolutionize and make their own of so much of the territory as they may inhabit. More than this, a majority of any portion may revolutionize, putting down a minority, intermingled with or near about them, who may oppose this movement. Such a minority was precisely the case of the Tories of our own revolution. It is a quality of revolutions not to go by old ideas or old laws; but to break up both, and make new ones" (Sandburg, WY II, p. 560).

One would conclude that by these words of 1848 Abraham Lincoln would sanction and legitimize the South's Declaration of Independence II, a parallel break from the oppressive North much as the colonies severed their ties with the mother country, Britain. But in the 1850s his position became radically opposite, and the reasons for such a seismic shift can only be speculated about, but in my view, explained by political considerations. As Abraham Lincoln was well-known as a political animal, always aware where political power was to be found, He directed all his efforts to raise himself out of this state of powerlessness to one of political clout.

As the issue of slavery became thrust into the public's attention by the activity of the abolitionists, and especially by Harriet Beecher Stowe's magnificent propaganda coup *Uncle Tom's Cabin*, Abraham Lincoln used it as a centerpiece in his debates with Stephen Douglas, making it a virtual national referendum. In doing so, he attracted enormous press coverage caught not only the public eye but also that of the powerful behind-the-scenes power brokers who used their political machines to maneuver this political wannabe and propel him into the most powerful political seat in the land… the presidency!

Now the hopes and aspirations of the Southerners for their independence, for their freedom, for their own self-determination, totally different from and opposite to the views of their oppressor, the North, Lincoln views as treason!

LINCOLN'S OBSESSION

When researching the life of Abraham Lincoln, the authoritative texts, almost without exception, relate a scene that haunted Lincoln for years to come. While on a trip down the Ohio River in 1841, they came upon a river craft transporting twelve negro slaves down South, chained to each other and to the boat ("strung together precisely like so many fish on a trot-line"). Fourteen years later, when he recalled this disturbing image, he described it as "a continual torment to me." That he should be disturbed by such an event that was quite commonplace in those times seems, to me, very surprising. In reading of his life, one would not suspect he was a man of delicate sensibilities who would be psychologically burdened by such a display. Somewhere in his upbringing lies the clue that made him view slavery as a morally indefensible institution. It was only as president, with unlimited power at his disposable, that he could and did address the issue with a seeming vengeance that only a dictator could possess. But we can only speculate whether the butcheries, described euphemistically as battles, had an unusually searing effect upon his brain and be "a continual torment to me." Apparently not, for he pursued his vision with a monomaniacal intensity, which would not be deflected by the many piles of corpses on the many battlefields. They died miserably and unnecessarily under the misunderstanding that it was their duty to "preserve the Union." And for what purpose did 1,000,000 Americans have to die? That four million slaves might be set free? What a preposterously exorbitant price!

DEBATER (THUMBNAIL SKETCH OF THE CIVIL WAR)

There is ample evidence concerning Abraham Lincoln to indicate to every reader that his life should be interpreted and studied primarily as a debater. Historical accounts reveal time and time again his willingness to debate any subject at any time with any one on his aim was not merely to score debating points but to dominate the discussion and win the contest decisively! His training as a lawyer, to construct a position with great care to convince an impartial body of the soundness of his case and to render a verdict favorable to his client. *Is the sine quae non* of Abraham Lincoln's life!

This success, however did not translate very well in his early political career where he had only a checkered success in the Illinois state legislature and the House of Representatives in Washington. Perhaps it is because of his criticism of the war with Mexico that he lost many political supporters. Whether this is true or not is immaterial, but he was in a state of limbo until his well-publicized debates with Stephen Douglas where he could again display his superior oratorical and debating skills. It is on this national stage that Lincoln regained his reputation as a major figure on the political scene, presenting his credentials to the nation that he was the best candidate to lead them in these times of turmoil. Backed by the political powers of the Eastern establishment his debating skills vaulted him into the White House.

Once there and, therefore, the most powerful man in the nation, he addressed the continuing major friction between the North and South over the issue of slavery. Typical of a clever lawyer he admitted that, while he could do nothing about slavery where it already existed, the government had the right to restrict its extension into the new territories! The South, recognizing his assertions as an attack upon their well-being and, perhaps more critically, on their survival, given the major importance of cheap slave labor in their economy, felt obliged to withdraw from the Union to survive! Taking their ideas right from the Declaration of Independence and, therefore, from all the philosophic input from Hobbes, Locke, Rousseau et al., the South asserted their moral right, i.e., that each and every individual human being possesses the inherent right to his/her own destiny toward self-determination and self-government, and that this moral right trumped or superseded any legal claims asserted by Lincoln!

Lincoln, ever the attorney, mounted a concerted attack upon this moral claim, insisting that his legal opinion over-rode all other assertions, becoming less than an impartial judge and jury, finding the South guilty of treason, and using his eminent power as commander-in-chief ordered the armed forces to arrest all persons of the South, bludgeon and kill them if they resist!

LINCOLN AND FORT SUMTER

In his first inaugural address Lincoln promised to avoid "bloodshed and violence" but left himself an escape clause: "unless it be forced on the national authority." But he also pledged to "hold, occupy and possess the property and places belonging to the government." Thus the report by Major Robert Anderson from Fort Sumter on March 5, 1861, presented Lincoln, a man of limited military experience, with a crisis upon which he procrastinated so long and made none. General-in-chief Winfield Scott recommended: "Evacuation seems almost inevitable if done before it is assaulted and carried," and any attempt to relieve the garrison "would require a force of 70,000 good and well-disciplined men." Although this evacuation was considered a military necessity, Lincoln viewed it as politically "ruinous." After prolonged and fruitless discussions the exasperated South fired on the Fort on April 12, 1861, and started the Civil War. Thus, much as children on the playground claiming "he hit me first" Lincoln could lay the blame of the War at the feet of the South, attempting, by historical accounts successfully to absolve himself of any responsibility! This line of reasoning is borne out by one of his most influential and critical friends Orville Hickman Browning who wrote to Lincoln before his inauguration: "In any conflict… between the government and the seceding states, it is very important that the traitors shall be the aggressors, and that they be kept constantly and palpably in the wrong. The first attempt… to furnish supplies or reinforcements to Sumter will induce aggression by South Carolina, and then the government will stand justified, before the entire country, in repelling that aggression, and retaking the forts." Having followed this scenario he told Browning, "The plan succeeded. They attacked Sumter—it fell, and thus, did more service than it otherwise could." He also responded to Gustavus Fox, "You and I both anticipated that the cause of the country would be advanced by making the attempt to provision Fort Sumter, even if it should fail; and it is no small consolation now to feel that our anticipation is justified by the result." Thus, the Fort, which had no military value served Lincoln's purposes eminently well. He afterward told congress, "no choice was left but to call out the war power of the Government; and so to resist force, employed for its destruction, by force, for its preservation." Uncontested surrender of the Fort would have created an appearance of groveling at the feet of Southern insurrection, an appearance he feared both from his party and the people of the North

An inflammable situation which required the utmost care and delicate handling, where one false move would almost certainly obliterate Unionism in South Carolina, Lincoln and his cabinet blundered into the war by allowing those who were concerned in saving face and giving the appearance of federal authority, afraid of being branded cowards and traitors, were pushed into the abyss by all these warlike imperious forces.

IF ONLY

A convincing argument can be made that a serious blunder was made by the British in surrendering the thirteen colonies to the upstart Americans both from an economic and political aspect and also from a humanitarian perspective. Had King George III the brutal instincts Abraham Lincoln he would have persisted in crushing the rebellion, hanging the leaders, and maintained the colonies as a British possession, ultimately to be incorporated into the more progressive British Empire and later to a more liberal British Commonwealth. In doing so the handling of the slavery issue would have been remarkably different than the horrendous effusion of blood that was seen as a result of the Civil War. The British handled the slavery issue in a more progressive, civilized fashion than as was seen under Lincoln's administration. Simply put, they declared slavery illegal and paid the slave owners the going rate for setting them free, i.e., for the loss of their "property." Had Lincoln a truly compassionate nature as he is portrayed to have had he might have settled the disagreement over slavery in a more humane and compassionate manner and the United States would not have wasted over 600,000 American lives and billions of dollars settling the issue otherwise. Sanity was a distinct feature of British governance in stark contrast to the volatile, virtually insane method of attempting to solve a virtually insoluble problem.

Contrary to its own economic interests England, in partnership with France's Napoleon III did not carry out a much-debated proposal to recognize the Confederacy and impose a truce that would break the Union's blockade of the South. To illustrate the economic importance of the South upon the British economy it should be pointed out that the American South supplied 75% of the raw cotton for the British textile industry, and by the summer of 1862, these imports had fallen to one-third of the 1860 level. This resulted in a "cotton famine" there and caused widespread unemployment. Lord John Russell, England's foreign minister, and William Gladstone, chancellor of the exchequer, both favored such recognition. It becomes obvious that if these leaders had sufficient firmness of purpose and concern for the economic well-being of their nation, they could have spared much unemployment, suffering, and hunger by the workers in the cotton textile industry. Their decisive actions would undoubtedly have had a secondary, but most certainly beneficial and humanitarian effect, namely, in preventing the unnecessary slaughter of over one-half million American lives, but more importantly from a philosophical and humanitarian perspective, it would have allowed the South to follow the principles of self-determination and create a second powerful, democratically run nation to emerge on this continent. If only!

LINCOLN THE BUNGLER

James G. Randall referred to the men of the 1850s as the "blundering generation as he viewed a series of blunders by incompetent politicians leading up to the Civil War. Under the understanding that the primary obligation of any politician is to do everything in his power to avoid wars we see that Abraham Lincoln failed in this regard. Mistakenly assuming a short duration for the conflict with the South, he called upon the loyal states 75,000 militiamen, "three month men" into service. But upon receiving a punch in the nose at Bull Run / Manassas he realized his miscalculation and called for 45,000 volunteers to serve for three years. Meeting in special session on July 4, 1861, the Congress authorized a call for 500,000 more men and another 500,000 after the first Bull Run.

In his first inaugural address, Lincoln grudgingly admitted: "Neither party expected for the war, the magnitude or the duration, which it has already attained."

The punch in the nose given to Abraham Lincoln at first Manassas (first Bull Run) made him realize he had blundered in thinking he could easily subdue the South with merely ninety-day recruits, and enraged his to demand a larger military force to crush the South. He failed to realize that his brothers in the South had virtually the same West Point education as those of the North, and that their generals and officers could accordingly organize their forces into efficient fighting machines ready to protect and defend the South's territories and perhaps even to go on the offensive!

Having been greatly embarrassed in the War of 1812–1814 major changes were made in America's military establishment by learning the art and science of warfare by study and exposure to European armies. Then the war with Mexico in 1846 gave the American generals and officers an opportunity to test their knowledge in real-life battlefield conditions. As a result, when the American Civil War broke out, both sides were experienced and well-seasoned in the art and science of war. Sadly all this knowledge led to a prolonged classic chess match that raged to and fro for four long bloody, painful, and costly years!

BUTCHER

If we accept the long-held premise that the institution of slavery is incompatible with the individualist and libertarian values common to dissenting Protestantism and the political thought of the Enlightenment, then the logical question must inescapably follow, "How do we convince our Southern brethren that the long-held habit of the exploitation of man by man… of one man 'owning' another man in perpetual bondage is wrongful and unacceptable by today's standards." Many words by many people were exchanged by both sides on this thorny issue as the South, ever resentful of the attacks upon their "peculiar institution," refused to accept the North's position.

However, just as Alexander the Great solved the very complex problem of the Gordian knot by taking out his sword and unraveling the knot by cutting it, so too did Abraham Lincoln solve the equally complicated issue of slavery in the South by taking out his sword and with the torch laid waste the South. None but a cold-blooded butcher could push his own people into the jaws of death and over the cliff and into the abyss. None but a callous son-of-a-bitch could then shed crocodile tears reading the casualty lists, of the tragic loss of so many "brave young men" when he himself had the ultimate power to stop the insanity, to stop the carnage, to stop the unnecessary effusion of blood! No wonder he seemed so depressed on so many occasions! Upon reading these lists only a man totally devoid of conscience would fail to be moved to tears of guilt and remorse.

Even granting the "unimaginable horrors" of slavery, the most significant question we must answer: is the evil of slavery worse than the slaughter of over 1,000,000 Americans, the devastation and ruin of cities North and South, with the enormous cost included? To win a minor victory of emancipation did Lincoln have to trash America to achieve the abolitionists' vision? This seems to me a grotesquely distorted sense of values.

In 1858, in one of his famous debates with Stephen Douglas, Lincoln predicted, after affirming the total wrongness of slavery that "I do not suppose that in the most peaceful way ultimate extinction would occur in less than 100 years at the least." Instead of a long, arduous, but peaceful, road to emancipation impatient Lincoln preferred the sword and gunpowder for more immediate resolution. The loss of so many lives seemed of minor significance and consequence, a mere bump in the road to freedom for the slaves!

LINCOLN AND RELIGION

In one of the books I read there was a description of his religious outlook, "like his father, he was reluctant to accept any creed. His parents' Baptist belief in predestination was deeply ingrained in his mind, though he felt more comfortable in thinking that events were foreordained by immutable natural laws than by a personal deity. To his cool analytical mind the ideas of the evangelists were less persuasive than those of the few local freethinkers, who gathered about the store cracker barrel and, when there were no customers in sight, engaged in speculation about the literacy of the Bible, the Virgin Birth, the divinity of Christ, and the possibility of miracles." Discussion of such issues was heresy in this rigid orthodox frontier community and inevitably reports of Lincoln's participation in these conversations leaked out. So damaging was the allegation that he was an "open scoffer at Christianity" that in his race for Congress in 1848 he was obliged to issue a formal denial; "that I am not a member of any Christian church is true' but I have never denied(?) the truth of the Scriptures, and I have never spoken with intentional disrespect of religion in general, or of any denomination of Christians in particular," and later added that he could never "support a man for office, whom I know to be an open enemy of, and scoffer at, religion."(A clever deceptive evasion!)

His stepmother is reported to have said, "Abe had no particular religion, didn't think of these questions at that time, if he ever did."

Much later in my reading, one writer observed that "Lincoln had no more religion than a cat." With these examples of Lincoln's lack of or disdain for established Christianity I am amazed at the profusion of religious references in his second inaugural address. It has the ring of being composed and uttered by a Baptist preacher rather than a secular, almost blaspheming president! Whence the sudden conversion? Some maintain it was an honest religious experience, a genuine conversion, an epiphany. Balderdash, say I! By hiding behind the protective shield of the Bible he deviously absolves himself of any and all responsibility for the carnage. It was "God's will."

ORIGIN OF THE SECOND INAUGURAL ADDRESS

In September 1864, to Mrs. Eliz P. Gurney (of the Society of Friends), Lincoln wrote: "The purposes of the Almighty are perfect, and must prevail, though we erring mortals may fail to accurately perceive them in advance. We hoped for a happy termination of this terrible war on before this; but God knows best, and has ruled otherwise... we must work earnestly in the best light he gives us, trusting that so working still conduces to the great ends he ordains. Surely he intends some great good to follow this mighty convulsion, which no mortal could make, and no mortal could stay."

Again it was "God's will."

The ultimate heresy (and malignancy) are revealed when Lincoln tells us that he would pursue the war even if he had to slaughter all the Southerners to achieve his goals when he says, "Yet if God wills (note the 'if') that it continue until all the wealth piled by the bondman's two hundred and fifty years of unrequited toil shall be sunk, and until every drop of blood drawn by the lash shall be paid by another drawn with the sword, as was said three thousand years ago, so still it must be said, 'The judgments of the Lord are true and righteous altogether.'" Amore brutal statement could not have been uttered by tyrant that has ever existed and I am shocked that the reportage of this speech showed no shock at its brutality! The war continued to drag on battle after battle, carnage after carnage, destruction piled upon destruction because "the Almighty has His own purposes." Man could not stop it because it was out of his hands! The ultimate clever lawyer's evasion.

LINCOLN AND RELIGION AND HIS SECOND INAUGURAL ADDRESS

No matter how hard the Founding Fathers tried to keep religion out of politics, i.e., out of official governmental activities (separation of church and state), or as Madison put it "the general government is proscribed from interfering, in any manner whatever, in matters respecting religion," it was conversely understood, or at least hoped for, religion would keep out of politics. Unfortunately, but especially in times of peril, there is a tendency for Christians to pray to God for his assistance and protection. When the nation lies exposed to its enemies it seems wise to take every opportunity to ensure divine blessings

Thus, contrary to the hopes of the Founding Fathers, religion has intruded itself into the political landscape. In 1812, Francis Scott Key, in our official anthem, buttressed Christian activism by uttering: "Praise the Pow'r that has made and preserv'd us a nation. Then conquer we must when our cause is just." Then during the Civil War, Julia Ward Howe composed the majestic and memorable "Battle Hymn of the Republic" with its biblical references to Isaiah 63:3 and Revelation 14:20. It was during WW II that "God Bless America" became the nation's unofficial national anthem, and during Truman's presidency that "under God" was added to the Pledge of Allegiance.

The historical accounts of the Civil War are replete with innumerable tragedies, but the greatest of these lies in the fact that its foundation was based upon the unquestioned premise that slavery was a Sin in the eyes of God! As a biblical dilettante I became flabbergasted to discover that this was not so, yet all the abolitionist groups, purportedly well-versed in biblical matters, insist to the world that it was! If anyone interested in the truth cares to look it up in the Bible he/she will discover that I am right. Therefore the question must arise. Were the abolitionists, in fact, really ignorant of the facts or were they deliberately lying through their teeth? The truth is, nowhere does the Bible criticize or proscribe the institution of slavery. It was a matter-of-fact occurrence and integral part of the society of that era. To my way of thinking, the ultimate tragedy lies in the fact that there existed no justification for this war and it should never have occurred!

Lincoln's second inaugural address continues the mentality that possessed those who first landed on these shores, that man's sufferings are all due to a direct punishment from God for our sins and, in this case, for the sin of slavery! And because the nation as a whole was complicit in that sin, so God was exacting the penalty of that sin, proportioning blood spilled by the soldiers' bullets and bayonets to that shed by the slavemasters' whips. A solidarity in sin made the punishment communal, uniting the nation in the suffering it had brought upon itself. Lincoln closed this one-sided debate by uttering "The judgments of the Lord are true and righteous altogether." No human dares challenge this statement, it comes from God himself! All that is missing, for modern-day congregations is for Lincoln to thump his Bible and shout Hallelujah! as do our evangelists. In that way he could proceed without analysis or moral introspection and carry out his butchery as if it were justifiable homicide.

Again we see a man who had virtually no religion cleverly use Christian allusions to support his political policies and war aims. In this speech he goes overboard in espousing the fundamental virtues found in Christian teachings: love, charity, mercy, compassion, humility, and selflessness. By this appeal to Christian tenets he would convince overwhelmingly his audience of his magnanimity and charity to the conquered South, but to me, it seems ironic if not hypocritical that he "got religion" at a convenient time, when his troops were finally crushing the Confederates and victory was assured. These remarkable attributes seemed nowhere in evidence when the war was beginning where he would conveniently overlook the biblical proscription, "Thou shalt not kill."

PROPAGANDA

PROPAGANDA AND THE CIVIL WAR

If we keep George Orwell's analysis in mind: "Who controls the past, controls the future, and who controls the present, controls the past," and dispassionately look at all the events surrounding the American Civil War, we discover this animal propaganda flourishing outrageously, first in the hands of the abolitionists and their cohorts then in the hands of the politicians, and lastly in the hands of the historians of the winning side, and who perpetuated the bullshit well-established by the other two.

Without a doubt the abolitionists carried off the biggest and most successful propaganda coup of the nineteenth century and perhaps of all time. By positioning themselves on the moral high ground, portraying and posturing as the embodiment of care, compassion and concern for the welfare of the downtrodden exploited Negro slave. Seizing upon the Declaration as the righteous angels of mercy righting the wrongs of slavery, they portrayed themselves as "all men are created equal"; they incessantly beat the Southerners over the head with it insisting such consideration be also given the slaves and by logical extension give them their freedom. The next step was a progressive escalation of the rhetoric in tone, volume, and frequency, a drumbeat of propaganda, insisting next that slavery was a sin in the eyes of God and it was the sacred mission of the abolitionists, of pure altruism, to wean the South from this monstrous habit. In later years, this technique of repeating lies and half-truths with urgency and intensity till achieved an appearance of veracity was used with great effect by a man name Joseph Goebbels. They, perhaps unknowingly but certainly with great effect, used the "triple-appeal" principle to stupendous effect.

But the harsh reality in studying the abolitionists with a sharp and dispassionate eye leads one to conclude that they were a malignant group of people, doing, heinous things, for truly evil purpose, all the while masquerading as pious activists in the service of God. They're hypocrites! activity, in my humble opinion, was not dispassionate altruism. They were keenly aware of the reality of political power, its ability to dictate to the masses from this ultimate seat of power—Washington and whoever controlled this power ruled the nation with an iron fist to bludgeon opponents into submission.

The designated torchbearer was found in the back woods of Illinois, a country lawyer and perennial aspiring politician with checkered success. Made famous with debating success against another notable, Stephen Douglas, Abraham Lincoln caught the eye of the eastern power establishment who brokered, primarily in smoke-filled rooms away from public scrutiny, this bumpkin, a dark horse long shot into the leading Republican candidate, displacing more experienced and qualified candidates. The three other presidential candidates received 2.8 million votes and Lincoln 1.8,39190; not a majority but Lincoln got 180 electoral votes, Breckenridge 72, Bell 39, and Douglas 12. Once in control of the levers of power Lincoln, the ostensible compassionate and of great magnanimity, confounded the experts by suspending basic freedoms because of wartime necessity and proceeded to mercilessly pursue and crush the South and devastate the country. Only a person of utter ruthless pragmatism could have achieved such a pinnacle of success. Lincoln was that man!

A necessary component of warfare is the use of propaganda to prepare and strengthen the minds of the populace, motivate and inspire our civilian and military forces, and undermine that of the opponents. Our reasons for battle must always be portrayed as of the highest moral orientation, filled with a sense of obligation and duty and portraying the enemy's motives as heinous, evil, and dangerous and deserving of their deaths. This is then followed by a sustained and persistent effort in the physical battle until we are triumphant and the enemy is utterly defeated. Once they have hurled themselves in battle, events carry them through the horrors until the enemy is justly slaughtered and vanquished.

THE USE OF PROPAGANDA TECHNIQUES DURING THE AMERICAN CIVIL WAR

The historians (a.k.a. the bullshitters) writing about the American Civil War spent an inordinate amount of time and energy portraying the North as embarking upon a noble crusade and the South as defending an evil practice—slavery. The North's heroic task is characterized as justifiable homicide to prevent a catastrophic calamity, the disintegration of the Union! Their crystal ball is 'crystal' clear that secession by the South would most certainly ruin that novel experiment in democracy ending in chaos. Bullshit! A supporting justification, some may view it as primary, not secondary, for this butchery, is the salutary effect of freeing the slaves, "an abomination in the eyes of God." Again, bullshit!

An equally important aspect in these propaganda wars (I am of the opinion that Joseph Goebbels learned the importance and effectiveness of propaganda techniques from the Northern peoples involved in the Civil War) was to denigrate the South as fighting (exclusively) to maintain this odious institution—slavery!

CONTRARIAN'S VIEW

In all my readings on Abraham Lincoln, slavery and the Civil War, and the attendant history, virtually no one has dared to present a contrary view to the received wisdom of that era. No one has had the boldness, temerity or nerve to challenge or swim against the tsunami of bullshit, the carefully crafted scenario originating from the political hacks of Lincoln's cabinet ("Now he belongs to the ages"—Edwin Stanton). It is here through early programming of the nation's mindset, then bolstered by the obsequious historians, Lincoln has achieved heroic stature, a moral crusader "to preserve the Union" by forceful, decisive action. Now we are told that he was perhaps our greatest president!

I beg to differ. The bodies of over 1,000,000 Americans, North and South, are a sad testament that belies such a preposterous assertion! So when all these people tell me all these praises of this man, I can only reply in my best New York vernacular: "Get outta here!" Or in my own hometown language: "Are you shittin' me?" Or in my best John McEnroe questioning of some adverse calls: "You can't be serious."

PROPAGANDA A LA MADISON AVENUE

Many of us assume that advertising techniques and mind-manipulating propaganda was of recent vintage, but the items from the past reveal that is not the case. For example, in preparation for the fourth Lincoln-Douglas debate in Charleston, Illinois, on September 1858, the city was decorated with flags and emblems, and most importantly, a banner eighty feet long stretched across the main street depicting "Old Abe Thirty Years Ago," showing Lincoln driving three yoke of oxen harnessed to a Kentucky wagon. At Maltoon, Lincoln's procession included a chariot of thirty-two young women representing the thirty-two states. Then in Galesburg, a banner "Small-fisted farmers, mud sills of society, greasy mechanics, for A. Lincoln." Here we see quite early in the nation's history the methods used on Madison Avenue, i.e., the high-pressure techniques of the advertising business.

PROPAGANDA AND THE SLAVERY ISSUE

Fugitive-slave narratives became useful tools in the propaganda wars to abolish slavery. The pattern of this narrative was virtually identical to the ones before: the slave is portrayed as suffering under the heavy burden of his or her oppression, and the impulses for liberty, freedom, and equality are so strong that they overwhelm the slave to make a break for freedom. Despite early failures, but with dogged persistence, he/she finally succeeds in obtaining his/her freedom, and, once secure, works tirelessly to advance the cause of freedom for all slaves, beginning with the autobiography slave-narrative, e.g., "The Narrative of the Life of Frederick Douglass."

When the object (abolition) was right, the abolitionists and their supporters concluded that the means (Civil War with its attendant butchery) could not be wrong. They were led to think they did their God and their country the most substantial service. But their recourse to violence reveals the bankruptcy of their capacity for reason and argument.

HBS

No other book had so dramatic an effect on the American consciousness, and consciences on the American psyche nor on American History as Harriet Beecher Stowe's epoch-making novel, *Uncle Tom's Cabin*. Abraham Lincoln's famous welcome to Stowe upon her visit to the White House, "So this is the lady who wrote that book that made this great war" attributes to her the major impact upon the nation's guilt that eventually led to that great conflagration, the Civil War. Throughout her life she repeatedly asserted that God had written this famous novel, and that she was merely his amanuensis. She declared that Uncle Tom's martyrdom came to her one day in church. Instead of all the world nodding knowingly, where were the Christian scholars who should have been shouting "Blasphemy"! God would have most assuredly disavowed any connection with such a preposterous secular production masquerading as a Christian epistle, a work that, however well-intentioned, galvanized the nation into hostile warring camps killing each other in the name of God. Had she not read the Ten Commandments? As a daughter of a minister, a sister of two, and the wife of yet another, she shows an abysmal lack of knowledge of the Bible, or was it a deliberate effort to ignore the Bible in order to achieve this propaganda coup.

As an amateur student of the Bible, I am puzzled to the point of amazement as to where the abolitionists found biblical support for their contention that slavery was evil or that slavery was a sin. In all of its voluminous writings nowhere does the Bible condemn the practice of slavery. All the reference acknowledge the practice and long existence throughout the nations of the Middle East that it was a matter-of-fact practice, and the biblical recommendations are that both slave and master should do their best to make friendly and respectful accommodations with one another. Nowhere does the Bible call slavery evil, and, most importantly, nowhere does it call slavery sinful! Yet with the repeated assertions, and they were deliberate lies, that slavery was a sin, they whipped the nation into a sufficient state as to bring about the greatest of calamities, the Civil War. It did not originate in the mind of Joseph Goebbels to originate this technique of repeating lies with sufficient frequency as to give it an appearance of verisimilitude. It was used to stupendous success by, an unlikely group, the compassionate Christian abolitionists and their cohorts, among them the celebrated Harriet Beecher Stowe.

When her father became the first president of Lane Theological Seminary in Cincinnati, Ohio, Harriet had an opportunity to visit Washington, Kentucky, in about 1850, and it is here that she obtained firsthand experience with that mostly Southern "peculiar institution," slavery. She was sufficiently moved by that exposure to the treatment of slaves by slave traders, masters, and overseers to write that world famous book *Uncle Tom's Cabin*. It first appeared in serial form in the National Era, and when that proved fantastically successful, in book form. This profoundly moving book, widely published and read, had an enormous impact upon the nation, convincing it of the monstrous evil of slavery and the urgent need to abolish the practice immediately.

Her book purports to give readers an honest glimpse of plantation life as she herself observed in Kentucky as if it were typical of the whole South. It is "about" characters we can identify with and who inhabited a world the reader considers to be socially, politically, and economically true to life. In truth her scenes are overdrawn exaggerations—maudlin sentimentality masquerading as truth. We see the unspeakable cruelty, oppressions, and sufferings inflicted upon nature's children by all the Southerners depicted as vicious and evil slave traders, overseers, and owners. Time and again she would return to her major theme—slavery was an abomination and sin against God—a fact that cannot be supported by the Bible.

In my opinion it was not an honest presentation of the reality of human experience. It was moreover a distortion by the overdrawn scenes deliberately designed to portray Southern whites in the worst possible light, as irredeemably corrupt and evil and the saintly slaves enduring the lash from their masters. Her scenes full of moral passion appeal to the soft compassionate nature of man's character and are the most powerful emotional portrayals against slavery. Tearful scenes, maudlin sentimentality trump dispassionate arguments to the contrary. *Uncle Tom's Cabin* is the most powerful and most enduring work of art ever written with its images seared into the brain; it is a work that psychologically manipulates human emotions to cry out against this foul assault on humanity—slavery.

It is in a class by itself, and because it moved the nation to a fever pitch eventuating in the slaughter of over 1,000,000 Americans, qualifying it as the greatest case of fratricide ever, elevates the book as the most successful piece of propaganda ever devised by man. It must have been the envy of the second most successful propagandist, Joseph Goebbels

If we are to second Abraham Lincoln's accolade that she brought about the Civil War that led to the abolition of slavery then on the other side of that same coin we must hold her equally responsible for the deaths of over 1,000,000 Americans. For much as a snowball can cause a disastrous avalanche, so did her book cause a cascade of events eventuating in the Civil War. In the philosophical debate of good and evil, the question arises what is more evil, the existence of slavery, or the deliberate slaughter of Americans to end slavery? The Bible can help us to resolve this dilemma. There can be found *no* commandment that says, "thou shalt not participate in that evil practice, slavery," but there can and is found in one of the Ten Commandments, "Thou shalt not kill!" Where was her Christian voice when Northern Christians and Southern Christians slaughtered each other? As a dyed-in-the-wool Christian she could safely hide behind this camouflage of compassionate humanitarianism, a true Christian concerned only with the welfare of the oppressed. In truth she was a meddlesome troublemaker rocking America's boat ending in disaster.

Writers and historians persist to this very day in using Christianity to support their claims. For instance Alfred Kazin in his introduction to her book says! "She certainly did reach hundreds of thousands of readers by shocking into awareness of the slave business… the buying and selling of slaves that violated every formal profession of Christianity," and "the outraged southerners sufficiently stung by Mrs. Stowe's indictment of their peculiar institution as a violation of Christianity." Even John Wesley called it "that execrable sum of all villainies." Was there not a slight defect in his knowledge of the Bible? Finally Mrs. Stowe's brother Edward (a clergyman) wrote in 1865, "Now that God has smitten slavery unto death, he has opened the way for the redemption and sanctification of our whole social system."

HBS SERMONIZING LIAR OR HYPOCRITE

As the daughter, wife and sister of ministers her view was unalterably fixed that Christianity and slavery could not coexist in America, that they were mutually exclusive entities and this became the major theme in her masterful work, *Uncle Tom's Cabin*. She took it upon herself not only to sermonize but also to propagandize to her fellow Americans to make them feel the onerous guilt of the "sin" of that evil institution slavery. Yet if one cares to go to the trouble to look up and research the question of slavery in the Bible, one will be surprised to discover not a single negative comment nor proscription against this institution. Then where did she acquire such an opinion if it did not exist in the Bible? Does that then not make her an outright and brazen liar, or at least a hypocrite?

Mrs. Stowe had great dramatic instincts and, combined with feminine compassion, was able to paint heart-rending scenes in the life of Uncle Tom. The idyllic hearth-side pictures of his home life clashing with the unspeakable cruelty done to him by his handlers engendered in the reader a moral revulsion and hatred toward the system, including the owners and their overseers. Then the emotional rupture of families, the unnatural tearing away of a child from its mother, of wife from husband, exposed the cruelty and heartlessness of slavery. Finally, the unnecessary and gratuitous beating to death of Uncle Tom for no apparent good reason exaggerates and reveals the ultimate and unfathomable cruelty of the system, and the whole book achieves the status as the most successful propaganda coup of the nineteenth century and perhaps of all time. To her Abraham Lincoln gave the accolade of, "So this is the lady who wrote the book that caused this great war."

It became painfully obvious to the world that this masterwork drained her of all her artistic energies for she was never to even approach the quality of workmanship in her subsequent works, which were abysmal failures. Or one might add sarcastically that she no longer received divine inspiration as she did for *Uncle Tom's Cabin*. To my consternation, I read where she apparently abandoned her pacifist principles and perhaps her Christian teachings (for she forgot that commandment, "Thou shalt not kill"). And she revealed to the world by saying, "Better, a thousand times better, open, manly, energetic war, than cowardly, treacherous peace." Are these not the ranting of a bloodthirsty tyrant and butcher and, most certainly not the utterances of a true Christian?

DOGS OF WAR

LINCOLN'S ENFORCERS (GOONS, MUSCLES, BRUTES, DOGS OF WAR)

Without these men, extensions of Lincoln's iron will, the outcome of the Civil War would surely have had a decidedly different outcome. Without generals who could extend and enforce the policies of the government Abraham Lincoln was merely a facade of government power, as was the idea of subduing the South to the North's yoke as a laughable if not a preposterous idea. Thus, it became acutely obvious and necessary for Lincoln to find the one general who could impose Lincoln's iron will upon the South. Lincoln finally, after a long and painful trial and error search, discovered three generals from Ohio, three Rottweilers, who could bring about the end of the world, as Southerners knew it, bringing the triumph of good and light over evil and darkness, yet no one describes the resultant death and destruction of this war as a pyrrhic victory, a cataclysm beyond understanding!

ULYSSES SIMPSON GRANT (1822–1885)

Americans seem to be perpetually infatuated by the idea of common people achieving great stature from humble beginnings, e.g., he and Lincoln were both born in log cabins. The son of a farmer and tanner, he was often described as short (five foot eight inches) sandy-haired, and a physically unprepossessing soldier who would never stand out in a crowd, one officer said he was "plain as an old shoe." The contrast between him and McClellan was as night versus day. Where flamboyant George McGlellan never travelled without a showy escort who loved to be greeted by his men with loud cheers and hats thrown into the air Grant was low key and inconspicuous: "the soldiers seem to look upon him as a friendly partner of theirs, not as an arbitrary commander… a pleasant salute to a good-natured nod in return seems more appropriate."

In battle, perhaps fortified by alcohol to give him courage, he fought like a Bulldog clamping his jaws down on his foe and never letting go until the body was lifeless. A man of attrition, grinding down his enemy to a fine dust with his superior numbers and materiel. Lincoln dismissed hid drinking problem by stating, "I can't spare this man; he fights."

WILLIAM TECUMSEH SHERMAN(1820–1888)

Having lived in the South he recognized the danger of the "young bloods" and the "awful fact" that victory required "that the present class of men who rule the South must be killed outright." Sherman may be best described as an unconventional warrior differing from Grant, and others in at least two respects. He did not follow established precedents for he eschewed frontal assaults where armies clashed directly. He would go around the set, fortified positions by repeated flanking movements thereby lessening his casualties and disorganizing the set positions of his enemies. He also discovered the necessity for "total" or "all-out" war where he would wage war not only on the opposing forces, but also on their infrastructure that supported them, munitions plants, transports, and finally upon the farms that fed the troops. If he could not beat them, he would starve them into submission. He did not play by the "rules" of the day!

(After the war there was no compassion left in him to extend to the Native Americans as he had given to the slaves. He did not extend protection for them in a civilized manner nor attempts to assimilate them into the mainstream.)

PHILIP HENRY SHERIDAN (1831–1888)

Rode up and down the Shenandoah Valley like a plague of locusts causing widespread death and destruction. Sandburg says, "Sheridan went dashing where the fire was most furious, waving his battle flag, praying swearing, shaking his fists, yelling threats and blessings, a demon in the flesh dedicated to fighting."

All three eventually became commanders of the U.S. Army.

Just as the Ten Plagues of Egypt constitute God's intervention on behalf of his people, "great acts of judgment" against Egypt, to bring about Israel's release from Egyptian slavery and servitude, so too did Abraham Lincoln cause the release by the three plagues of Grant, Sherman, Sheridan et al., to devastate the South, crushing them and causing the eventual release and emancipation of the Negro slaves from Southern bondage.

In reading of the depredations of Lincoln, and his alter egos Grant, Sherman, and Sheridan.

I am reminded of the image of the Four Horseman of the Apocalypse as described in the Book of Revelations. The figure representing conquest rides a white horse; war, a red horse; famine, a black horse; and death, a pale horse. Just as in the Bible these four are the biblical equivalent bringing about the "apocalypse" or final catastrophe that comes at the end of the world as they rained death and destruction upon the South. The Book of Revelations described the final triumph of good over evil, of Jesus over Satan, and the message is clear that despite all adversities, salvation will be achieved through the intervention of God.

FOUR HORSEMEN

Curiously Lincoln, Grant, Sherman and Sheridan all were born within 200 miles of one another. Was there something in the water in Ohio and Kentucky that made these men such formidable warriors? Lincoln, as commander-in-chief of the Armed Forces, ordered and coordinated his forces through a chain of command, provided his forces with all their military needs, but left virtually all military decisions to his generals (with an occasional prodding). By doing so he allowed them maximum freedom to take immediate advantage of any and every circumstance that offered them opportunity. They planned their battles beforehand, but as events evolved, they adapted and altered these plans accordingly to deal with these realities. These actions were almost instinctive, accepting, and exploiting the unexpected behavior of their enemies through adaptations to changing circumstances. Lincoln, in Washington, took care of and conducted national diplomacy, finances, and strategy ("politics") while they took care of military affairs.

This shows that they did not get bogged down in their minds with elaborate textbook theories as taught at West Point. Time after time their battles were characterized by pushing their troops relentlessly toward victory, scarcely giving themselves or their opponents time to recover before pushing the attack again! Their "total warfare" was not only to destroy the enemy militarily but also to destroy his will to fight to crush them totally Grant, before Richmond, Sherman in Georgia, and Sheridan in the Shenandoah Valley, all contributed in squeezing the Confederacy and bring about total unconditional surrender.

Some say that the South still had a fondness for a united America, as they exhibited a slavish observation of the Fourth of July and Washington's birthday, but I insist it was more than that; it was moreover a love of the philosophical concepts of liberty, freedom and self-determination, ideas upon which the nation was founded. They were not in love with the nation, but with Lockean concepts of man's natural God-given natural rights to individual freedom and as exemplified in the Declaration of Independence and the Constitution! But Abraham Lincoln, with his limited education and mentality of a backwoods, barroom brawler would impose his iron will upon the nation butchering all those who espoused such a quaint concept of individual liberty and freedom to choose.

CHARLES A. DANA 1819–1897

Despite his stature as a prominent figure in nineteenth century journalism and after fifteen years as managing editor of Horace Greeley's mighty newspaper, the New York Tribune, his brilliant incisive mind did not save him from being fired by Greeley for his hawkish outlook on the Civil War. Dana was known to favor an all-out effort to prosecute the war.

As special assistant to the secretary of war, Edwin M. Stanton, his job was to discreetly spy upon Ulysses S. Grant's rumored drinking problem and, therefore, his competency to command, the Union army. This most crucial mission would, thus, determine the future of Grant and affect the outcome of the entire war.

His reports to Stanton were almost always favorable with many glowing in his admiration of the man. "I remember distinctly the pleasant manner, straightforward cordial and unpretending." Later after Grant's death he would summarize. "The most modest, the most disinterested, the most honest man I ever knew with a temper that nothing could disturb and a judgment that was judicial in its comprehensiveness and wisdom. Not a great man except morally; not an original or brilliant man, but sincere, thoughtful, deep and gifted with courage that never faltered."

His reporting on Grant during the successful Chattanooga campaign led to Lincoln's naming Grant overall commander of all the Union armies.

Because of his militant attitude toward the South and because he agreed with Lincoln in his assessment of Grant. "I can't spare him; he fights," he failed to faithfully alert Washington for this might have ended Grant's military career. Perhaps he had the notion that, with careful supervision, Grant's drinking could be controlled sufficiently to not interfere with his fighting courage.

The sharp contrast in military success between Ulysses S. Grant's progression from triumph to triumph and the ineptitude of the generals who preceded him has made historians ascribe to Grant a particular genius for waging war. Abraham Lincoln, coming from a backwoods environment, had a better understanding of the man as he encouraged the man: "Hold on with a bulldog grip, and chew and choke as much as possible." Again, when others attempted to get rid of Grant for drunkenness in battle, Lincoln gave him another vote of confidence by saying, "I can't spare the man. He fights!" To ascribe to Grant qualities of genius for what comes easily and naturally to a barroom brawler is an over-analysis of the events. War, as in a barroom brawl, presents issues but on a much larger scale. In a barroom fight, the issues are clearly understood and presented. All that is required is the resolution of the conflict, here and now. Only cowards back down, Shakespeare's Macbeth enunciated it eminently well as he said, "Lay on MacDuff, And damned be him that first cries, Hold enough!"

One way or another, the issues are resolved.

WAR

TERRORISM

In Grant, Lincoln had a commander whom he liked and trusted. An unpretentious man, not flamboyant as McClellan, simple and direct, endeared him to the president. "General Grant is a copious worker and a fighter, but a very meager writer and telegrapher... he doesn't cry or bother me. He isn't shrieking for reinforcements all the time. He takes what troops we can safely give him... and does the best with what he has got."

But ever the political animal Lincoln picked officers for several subordinate positions who were not favored by Grant. For instance, Benjamin Butler, despite his well-known incompetence remained at the head of the army of the James because he had a powerful following among Radical Republicans, and Franz Sigel, who had minimal military skills but was a favorite of German-Americans, was chosen to head the Union forces in the Shenandoah Valley.

Saddened and depressed by Grant's casualties in the Battle of the Wilderness (14,000) and in Spotsylvania (17,500) Lincoln took heart in Grant's determination. "I propose to fight along this line if it takes all summer." His was in sharp contrast to previous generals, willingness to withdraw after each engagement with the enemy and lick their wounds and regroup, whereas Grant went on to launch a new offensive. Lincoln is reported to have said during the battle of the Wilderness, "The great thing about Grant is his perfect coolness and persistency of purpose... he is not easily excited... and he has the grit of a bulldog! Once let him get his 'teeth' in, and nothing can shake him off." He was quite pleased to have a general who shared his determination to destroy and the obliterate the Confederate armies.

Mary Todd Lincoln assessment was totally at odds with her husband's, she often said of Grant. "He is a butcher, and is not fit to be at the head of an army."

In August of 1864, Sherman wrote: "War is the remedy our enemies have chosen... And I say let us give them all they want... not a sign of let-up, no cave in till we are whipped or they are... The only principle in this war is, which party can whip. It is as simple as a school-boy's fight and when one or the other party gives in, we will be the better friends."

Terrorism as we now understand it is to inflict such a psychological impact upon the enemy, military, and civilian, as to bring about the total collapse of resistance to the attacking armies. By undermining the support system that enables the soldiers to perform in the field this weakens the military's ability to perform to their maximum abilities. This can be achieved by applying tactics of extraordinary viciousness and brutality upon the civilians.

Captain B. H. Liddell Hart, the noted British historian called Sherman "brilliant" as "he came to see and exploit the changing conditions of warfare produced by mechanical and scientific developments." He tells us, "While Grant's primary objective was the enemy army, Sherman's was the seizure of strategic points. Atlanta, the base of the Confederate army opposing him in Georgia, was not only the junction of four important railways, but also the source of vital supplies." It was "full of foundries, arsenals and machine shops," as well as being of great importance psychologically as a symbol, and he held that "its capture would be a death knell to the Confederacy." Sherman's "strategy" found traction "in the paralyzing and demoralizing shock effect on the opposing armies and peoples simultaneously." "His unchecked march through the heart of the South, destroying its resources, was the most effective way to create and spread a sense of helplessness, that would undermine the will to continue the war." Would not these revelations qualify Sherman as one of the earliest exponents of the strategy the world recognizes as "terrorism?" In Sherman's time it was recognized as a brilliant tactic, but today we tend to frown on it as a reprehensible use of violence and brutality to achieve a political end!

Hart also said "the prime canon of military doctrine has been that the destruction of the enemy's main forces on the battlefield constituted the only true aim in war." Thus, the concept of "total war" was a revolutionary break with traditional thinking

Terrorism—in 480 BC the Persian army exhibited extraordinary brutality upon the defeated army of Athens, not only by merely destroying the army in the field but also by tearing down the venerable shrines held dear to the Greeks, those symbols of Greek culture. Thus, the concept of "terrorism" is not of recent origin, and one might argue had been resurrected by Sherman during his march through Georgia.

Superior manpower and resources are useless unless accompanied by energetic mental preparedness to hurl your forces at the enemy, a struggle to the death. It was not until the discovery by the North of aggressive leadership and Bulldog tenacity in Grant, Sherman, and Sheridan did the North start to gain some traction against the Southern forces.

QUESTION?

If we are to discuss and debate the more profound philosophical concept of the "morality of war" can we describe the American Civil War as a "just war," a war in which "right" was in confrontation of what we may term as definitely or irrefutably "wrong?" Was it a war that simply had to be fought no matter what amount of death suffering and bloodshed had to be endured? To my way of thinking this would be a resounding *no*! The catastrophic consequences of this War exceeds, in its short four years, those of all of America's wars, foreign and domestic, from the beginning of this nation's birth following the Revolution, right up to the twenty-first century! It could only be prosecuted by a rigid, fiendish, unbending megalomaniac with dictatorial tendencies, and his name is Abraham Lincoln! But first we must undertake the Sisyphean task and disabuse the nation of the bullshit that his actions were noble and were solely to "preserve the Union." As early as 1858, in his debates with Stephen Douglas, he clearly reveals his mania to sacrifice between 600,000 and one million Americans and billions of dollars just to liberate four million slaves!

CAIN

The Bible tells us of the first case of the murder when Cain killed Abel (Genesis 4:10) But the Lord said, "Your brother's blood calls to me from the ground. What have you done? You are hereby banished from this ground which you have defiled with your brother's blood." Where is the equivalent outrage as this in regards to the blood of 600,000 murdered "brothers" spilled all over the thousands of acres of American soil?

DECLARATION OF WAR

Despite the fact that the Constitution clearly gives Congress the final authorization in declaring war, a certainty supported by one of the Founding Fathers, George Washington, when he became President, "The Constitution vests the power of declaring war with Congress, therefore, no expedition of importance can be undertaken until after they shall have deliberated on the subject and authorized such a measure." There have been many breeches to this understanding as many "wars" have been declared without these courtesies by various and several presidents on numerous occasions. These declarations were, therefore, a violation and a travesty with respect to the letter of the Constitution and, unfortunately, a too frequent occurrence. Most violators claimed executive privilege insisting that particular situation a "threat to national security" and a "national emergency," thereby justifying swift action.

Abraham Lincoln's presidency represents the brutal reality of the triumph of might over right, of totalitarian oppression over individual freedom. It is individual freedom that matters more than anything on this earth. He, too quickly, rejected any suggestions of laborious and protracted compromise and negotiations with the South over the issue of slavery, but resorted to the quick expediency of military might believing in the supremacy of his ninety-day recruits. The punch in the nose at Bull Run / Manassas quickly disabused him of that ridiculous assumption He, too late, found himself on the slippery slope to a disastrous conflict worthy of the nomenclature of Armageddon and, smarting from the punch in the nose, he as the dictator that he truly was, seized the levers of power without even a token nod toward the existence of the legislature, and proceeded to set in motion policies designed to mercilessly crush the South.

BLOWING IN THE WIND

Nowadays when I hear the lyrics by Peter Paul and Mary's song "Blowing in the Wind... How many deaths will it take till we know that too many people have died," I have come to associate it with the killing fields of the American Civil War. My initial readings concerning the casualties of this War tell us that approximately 300,000 soldiers died. Later that was revised to 600,000. Lately, and perhaps finally, the January 30–February 6, 2006, issue of *U.S. News and World Report* informs us that the losses for the Union were 646,392, and for the Confederacy 335,524. Further, in the "total war" it is said that 50,000 civilians also perished! My consternation is boundless! It means that 1,000,000 American boys had to be killed to satisfy Abraham Lincoln's lust for solving the minor issue of slavery! The butchery of over 1,000,000 civilized, advanced young men just to free from bondage 4,000,000 illiterate, backward, savages is unconscionable. Could they not make more of an effort, other than brainless butchery, to solve a minor disagreement between the capitalist, industrial North, and the agrarian, aristocratic South?

It obviously required leadership of outstanding and exemplary qualities—to negotiate, to compromise, to deal with differences, to give and take, to yield on some points, but stand firm on others—all the while progressing to a bloodless solution, imperfect though it may be, but one that both sides could live with. Abraham Lincoln was *not* that man! With the self-righteous arrogance of a moralist and idealist, he impatiently imposed his will upon the nation, not stopping till victory was assured, even if he had to kill every Southerner to do so. The fact that he had killed many of the "best and the brightest" of that era seems to have escaped the notice of all the historians, and all the observers, and all the pundits. The American Civil War was an unmitigated catastrophe upon the nation and upon the world, yet no one seems to have noticed or cared. Only a few of these "best and brightest" survived the "American Holocaust." Among these was the noted jurist Oliver Wendell Holmes Jr., who, though wounded, three times managed to survive and serve with distinction on the United States Supreme Court. The next logical question is, how many others of such superior endowments and talents, out of this million, had their lives brutally cut short of fulfillment in this stupid war, and wasted, all because a group of compassionate zealots (abolitionists) who succeeded, through their incessant machinations, to put an unyielding brute upon the throne of the United States, Abraham Lincoln! Don't let exterior appearances fool you. Behind this benign exterior of a kind benevolent, avuncular man lay the heart of a brutal avenging angel of death intent on imposing his inflexible iron will upon the nation!

WAR DEATHS

Here in the twenty-first century the American populace seems squeamish and uneasy at the ever-escalating death toll in Iraq numbering less than 3,000 over a three-year period. There is an undercurrent of dissatisfaction verging on audible rumblings over this seemingly obscenely large number of dead and a noticeable cry of "bring the boys home" is heard. The question in my mind that bothers me so profoundly is, why did *not* the American people recoil in horror during the American Civil War when battle after battle after battle filled the newspapers with lists of dead numbering quite commonly in the 5,000–10,000 each, and some even higher? Again and again and again they were bludgeoned into silence by the numerous accounts of horrendous bloodletting and carnage, biting their tongues as their leaders insisted the "nation must be preserved," promising that the end of the war was near at hand! If we but persevere just a little more, peace is just around the corner.

INEVITABLE WAR?

Some historians assert that the Civil War was an inevitable occurrence, one that was unstoppable no matter what. The noted historian Arthur Schlesinger Jr., in a *New York Times Magazine* book review, is one of these as he is quoted: "The North's moral disgust over slavery.... made the Civil War necessary and inevitable." I beg to differ. Surely people more adept and knowledgeable in conflict resolution, those more willing to compromise or, as Churchill put it... Jaw, jaw, jaw, is better than war, war, war" could have been instrumental in averting this major catastrophe. A cerebral, rather than an angry, emotional, solution *would have obviated the carnage that* we euphemistically call the American Civil War. Anything would have been better than this calamitous, horrendous bloodbath!

Bernard de Voto said, "Whether or not the war was inevitable, the crisis was." He felt that the conflicts had to be solved but the fact that "they were not solved short of war is our greatest national tragedy." Then there is Sydney Hook who opined, "If the war was inevitable, it was tragic. If it was not inevitable, it was even more tragic." Then there is Ambrose Bierce, the Union soldier turned author and acerbic critic, who characterized the Civil War as "a murderous enterprise, without uplift, without virtue, and without purpose." Lastly, I like George Bernard Shaw's profound utterance: "Peace is not only better than war, but infinitely more arduous."

STUPIDITIES

The American Civil War will always be remembered as such even though it has been given several names and various descriptions: the War Between the States, the War of Northern Aggression, and Lincoln's War. To my way of thinking they all fail to describe the true essence of the altercation and disagreement; it has all the features of a family feud for it brings to mind the oft-told story of that between the Hatfields and McCoys. Upon looking into a dictionary you will find "feud" defined as "a lasting quarrel between families or clans marked by violent attacks undertaken for revenge." As the Hatfield-McCoy feud began innocently with a simple and stupid incident, it erupted over the attempted elopement of John Hatfield and Rosanna McCoy, so too did the American Civil War begin with a stupid and simple incident—the issue of slavery and its extension into the new territories. Both "feuds" careened out of control as events were overtaken by hotheads intent on doing bodily harm to their fellow Americans. Passions are allowed to run amok without calm reasoning to dampen the attacks, which bring about retaliation which brings about counterretaliation, and the cycle persists as a perpetual-motion machine. Unfortunately, it is only when the fighting is all over that the combatants look over the carnage and come to assess and analyze calmly the whole scenario. Only one conclusion is possible: man, through his uncontrolled, animal passions, behaves stupidly!

So too it was with the American Civil War where this "family feud" run by stupid people and letting events careen out of control, but not having the sense to stop the madness until too late, when the populace was almost obliterated and the cities virtually destroyed, and the fighters were too punch-drunk to continue!

PYRRHIC VICTORY

If ever there was a Pyrrhic victory mention of the Civil War in America qualifies as a prime example of that appellation since the original in 300 BC. For in that year Pyrrhus, king of Epirus, was involved in yet another war. Looking down upon his catastrophic losses in his victory at Asculum he is said to have uttered, "Another such a victory and I shall be ruined." So too it was with Abraham Lincoln and the Civil War! Lincoln, the Great Uncompromiser, pursued and slaughtered the South with a ferocity unheard of, sacrificing Northern troops, costing billions of dollars in the process, and leaving the nation devastated. And now we are left with the eternal bullshit that the abolition of slavery was a high moral crusade, a pursuit of a high noble cause, and the reality of massive death and destruction is glossed over and forgotten.

Let me quote from Carl Sandburg's six-volume masterpiece on Lincoln, a most poetic utterance, "Killed in action or dead from wounds and disease were some 620,000 Americans, 360,000 from the North, 160,000 from the South… planted in the tomb of the earth, spectral and shadowy, blurred and discordant in their testimonies for posterity as to why they fought the war and cut each other down in the heyday of their youth. They were a host. They were phantoms never absent from Lincoln's thoughts. Possibly from that vanished host, rather than from the visible and living, Lincoln took his main direction and moved as though the word 'reconciliation' could have supreme beauty if he could put it to work."

Thus Lincoln achieved a pyrrhic victory; his acolytes persist in portraying his actions as a moral crusade and, in the eyes of the world, justifiable homicide in order to bring the recalcitrant Southerners back into the fold, whatever was left of them!

JUSTIFIABLE HOMICIDE?

The defenders of the American Civil War portray the necessity of such drastic action on the premise that not to do so would have proved catastrophic, that the concept of allowing several states to voluntarily exit from the Union could and would not be permitted. They claim that if it were allowed then the novel experiment of democracy, or as Lincoln put it, "the last best hope of earth," would fail disastrously. Bullshit! This theory is pure fabrication, woven out of this air for the credulous and simple-minded, to justify the horrendous carnage that occurred to give a plausible explanation for the necessity of such brutal effusions of blood and treasure. To them, it was justifiable homicide, but it was a big fat lie! It was subterfuge! Their crystal-ball gazing and prognostications was designed to mislead the public to get them to believe their cause to be a noble one worthy of unanimous nationwide support.

In my humble opinion, the two severed parts of the nation, having a similar Anglo-Saxon heritage, the one-half financial, industrial, and capitalistic, the other agrarian with aristocratic pretensions, would have both survived and prospered in their own way, establishing a modus vivendi and peaceful coexistence. These two dissimilar yet utopian nation's growths would not have been retarded or stunted, as was the singular nation after the War with the loss of over 1,000,000 industrious souls. The energy of these wasted men would have contributed enormously to the robust expansion and explosion of a bountiful America. Unfortunately hotheaded butchers controlled the levers of governmental power and they steered the nation over the cliff and into the abyss of carnage and desolation; and with their clever manipulations made the aggressors smell like roses, making Abraham Lincoln the virtual incarnation of Jesus Christ and a secular saint, and the nation believed them!

CAUSES

CAUSES OF THE AMERICAN CIVIL WAR

To explain the causes of the American Civil War one need only to look at the Revolutionary War to see the similarities and parallelisms. The pioneer, self-reliant can-do attitudes of the nascent industrializing North clashed with the aristocratic pretensions of the mother country, Britain, and subsequently with those of the South who maintained this attitude even after the break, primarily because manual labor was done by the slaves, an activity felt beneath their dignity and demeaning. Once these con artists seduced the South into believing that (1) a Union of their forces was necessary to oust the exploiter, Britain, and (2) that once liberated the thirteen colonies would enjoy an explosion of political, economic, and cultural flowering of a virtual utopia. It was left for a later date and a later leader when the aristocratic South would be taken down a peg from their lofty perch by introducing them to the harsh reality of capitalism by applying gunpowder and cold steel in the American Civil War. No longer would their world be built on the backs of slave labor. No longer would they sip their mint juleps on their porches with ease and comfort with a confidence that all was well on the plantation. Death and destruction soon disabused them of that notion and turned their world upside down when the nineteenth century equivalent of the Four Horsemen of the Apocalypse: Lincoln, Grant, Sherman, and Sheridan butchered, burned, and destroyed everything in their paths and left the land desolate.

PRESERVE THE UNION

Lincoln was not above using the technique of "imaginative horror" in his arguments and, using his crystal ball, predicting economic disaster, political chaos and the ultimate fearful consequence, i.e., final collapse of what we know as the United States of America. Thus, the rallying cry "the Union must be preserved" to justify his ruthless suppression of the South's legitimate Declaration of Independence, phase II, or "Southern style." Conclusion? Thus, a case of justifiable homicide! Using such dire prognostications he convinced the nation and rallied it to defend the well-established principle origination from Madison's Federalist No. 59 "that every government ought to contain in itself the means of its own preservation." But this flies in the face of the also well-established philosophical principle enunciated by John Locke upon which the original Declaration is based, i.e., that government exists by the consent of the governed and, if a significant number of its citizens wish to form another form of government, they most certainly have the right to do so. This is supported by Hamilton's Federalist No. 22, which states, "The streams of national power ought to flow immediately from that pure, original foundation of all legitimate authority," (consent of the people). Thus, we see that Lincoln interpreted the Constitution as a document carved in stone, allowing no modification. It was a perfect production in "framing government for posterity" and Lincoln was the man to enforce its terms to the letter! He did not win over the hearts and minds of the South; he maintained the physical union but a permanently scarred and resentful one. A memorable line to this effect is from Hamilton's Federalist No. 1: "For in politics, as in religion, it is equally absurd to aim at making proselytes by fire and sword."

During Lincoln's First Inaugural Address he declared, "I hold that, in the contemplation of universal law and of the Constitution, the Union of these States is perpetual." At this point, it is mentioned, a cheer arose from the crowd.

As commander-in-chief and sworn to faithfully execute the laws, with the sweeping authority invested in the office, turned to military force as the final answer to secession, he said, "It became necessary for me to choose whether, using only the existing means, agencies and processes which Congress had provided, I should let the Government fall at once into ruin or whether availing myself of the broader powers conferred by the Constitution in cases of insurrection, I would make an effort to save it, with all its blessings, for the present age and for posterity."

To counter this opinion a more persuasive psychological argument would be in characterizing the secessionists as "freedom fighters" for that is precisely what they were!

SAVE THE UNION!

In contrast with the voluminous writings of the professional historians and other worshippers at the shrine of that secular saint Abraham Lincoln only Gore Vidal among writers of stature had the temerity to imply a criticism of Abraham Lincoln and his conduct in relation to the American civil War. "In order to save the Union he first had to destroy it." After much reflection upon this statement, I have come to the unalterable conclusion that he did not have to save the nation nor did he have to destroy it. Using a defective crystal ball he (Lincoln) came forth with the dire prediction that, should the nation be rent asunder by the actions of the South, a catastrophic and cataclysmic event would surely ensue, the death of that novel experiment—democracy. Through this frightening vision he galvanized the nation into the mightiest and nastiest war machine ever assembled on this earth to date. He with Grant, Sherman, and Sheridan became the modern equivalent of the Four Horsemen of the Apocalypse, spreading death and destruction over the whole nation! Nothing and no one was spared in their mania to subjugate the South.

    A study of Abraham Lincoln's remarkable success as a backwoods lawyer reveals him to be a clever and devious attorney always careful to craft his argument to appeal to the jury. With regards to the Civil War he had to be careful not to allow the true cause of the war to dominate the conversations and debates else he could not have persuaded the nation to pursue the war as vigorously as he would like. Had the nation been aware that the true cause of the war was the issue of slavery, and its disproportionate political and economic impact, he would have failed in his attempt to subdue the South. He, therefore, as a clever magician and prestidigitator focused the nation's attention on "saving the Union," the heroic struggle of good versus evil, of noble against the ignoble, of the well-intentioned against those who were not. The oft-repeated lie "save the Union" became the battle cry in all its permutations and combinations. As someone said, these actions were necessary."If the Ship of State was not to go over the cataract whose thunders ahead shook the air." This is the kind of propaganda that hurled the nation over the precipice and into the valley of death that we know as the American Civil War.

Let us look carefully at the clever use of the words "Union" and "nation" in some of Lincoln's subsequent speeches. In his first inaugural address he mentioned "union" twenty times, but the "nation" not once! In his first message to Congress on July 4, 1861, he used the word "union" thirty-two times and the "nation" three! And in his second inaugural address in 1865, he spoke of the challenge from the South seeking to dissolve the "union" and the North accepting the challenge to preserve the "Union," couching it in terms of a noble crusade. And finally, in the Gettysburg Address, he mentioned the "Union" not once, but spoke of the "nation" five times in regards to a "new birth of freedom." Yet no historian mentions, as Gore Vidal did, that "to preserve the Union he first had to destroy it." In this monomaniacal pursuit did he have to kill so many Americans to achieve this goal? Was this the only avenue open to resolve this dilemma? Could not someone of more statesmanlike qualities have negotiated a less bloody solution? But conciliation was nowhere to be found in the make-up of this brutal dictator! Only the iron fist!

CAUSES

1) Humanitarian—slavery was an odious practice
2) Philosophical—"equal"
3) Economic—democratic free-labor capitalism versus slave-labor plantation agriculture
4) Emotional—"preserve the Union," a sacrosanct entity to be worshipped and not rent asunder

PRESERVE THE UNION

In an attempt to justify the extreme measures that the North had to undertake to subdue the South, Abraham Lincoln attempted to portray the struggle in a larger, more philosophical context. "The issue," he said, "embraces more than the fate of these United States. It presents to the whole family of man the question of whether a constitutional republic, or democracy—a government of the people by the same people—can or cannot maintain its territorial integrity against its own domestic foes." Unfortunately, Lincoln was handicapped by his own narrow legalistic mind which prevented him from rising above it to appreciate the deeper philosophical Lockean principles imbedded in America's Declaration of Independence and Constitution. The Founding Fathers had signed, according to Lincoln's understanding, a binding legal document that committed all subsequent generations to keep the Union intact forever, and he, Abraham Lincoln, the lowly backwoods attorney from Springfield, Illinois, would see to it that these terms would be adhered to and abided by, even if he had to kill everyone who dared disagree with his opinion! Lincoln's interpretation of the Articles (1781) of Confederation and Perpetual Union to mean exactly what it said and as a lawyer insisted that the South live up to this agreement. To him it was not, as some historians believe, only an alliance among thirteen sovereign states, more like NATO. He would not allow them to abrogate the original document, thus, in my opinion, acting as the most uncompromising villain, drunk with the power of an attorney.

To give the War a patina of legitimacy and credibility it had to be couched in terms of dire consequences, i.e., the survival of the Republic was at stake! Shelby Steele supports this view by stating that a war of survival grants moral authority.

MINORITY ANTIWAR VOICES

Despite some powerful and influential voices in favor of letting the South to secede peacefully, the overwhelming number of impassioned advocates of war and Union (at any cost) drowned them out. The illustrious Winfield Scott, who favored Union even though a Southerner, had no illusions about subduing the South militarily. While many believed the conflict would be short Scott opined that the conflict would in fact last at least three years. An excellent article published in the Atlas and Argus, an Albany, New York newspaper on January 12, 1861, recommending peaceful secession had no influence on the nation and predicted "the war spirit will take possession of the populace and hurry us and the country on to ruin."

To his everlasting credit, William Lloyd Garrison, the most outspoken, the most determined and vehement of firebrands, who originally insisted on "abolition of slavery, now!" reconcile at the thought of "vindicating the sovereignty by the sword" or "extorting allegiance from millions of people at the cannon's mouth." He was one of the few dispassionate analysts who looked into his crystal ball and saw horrendous carnage. Others especially those in political power were determined to wreak vengeance upon their Southern brothers. Anger triumphed over reason and sanity. He alone had the sensible vision and said, "The people of the North should recognize the fact that THE UNION IS DISSOLVED" and act accordingly.

In Michael H. Hart's book "The 100: A Ranking of the Most Influential Persons In History," he does not include America's secular saint Abraham Lincoln. His first consideration in this analysis he questions, "Was not the freeing of some 3,500,000 slaves a major accomplishment?" His reply! "Indeed it was," but then he follows dismissively with "However, in retrospect, we see that the forces throughout the world-working toward the abolition of slavery-were irresistible. Many countries had abolished slavery even before Lincoln took office, and within sixty-five years of his death, most other countries did so. The most that Lincoln can be credited with accomplishing is having hastened the process."

The second consideration for inclusion here was. "Still it might be asserted that Lincoln chief accomplishment was in holding the United States together in the face of secession of the southern states." Again this assertion too is trivialized by, "But it was the election of Lincoln that touched off the 'secession' nor is it clear that the North would have failed to win the Civil War if someone other than Lincoln had been president… with (their) great advantage in population, and even greater one in industrial production."

Then, to me, the clinching argument that shows the tragic folly of Lincoln's murderous pursuit of his bloody objective is the paragraph: "Even if the North had not prosecuted the Civil War to a successful conclusion, the overall course of history might not have been greatly altered. The bonds of language, religion, culture, and trade between the North and South were very great, and it seems probable that they would have eventually reunited. If the period of disunity had lasted for twenty years—or even for fifty years—it would still be a minor incident in world history. (It should also be remembered that even without the South, the United States would now be the fourth most populous nation on earth and still the leading industrial power)."

WAR AND ANTIWAR BY ALVIN AND HEIDI TOFFLER, LITTLE, BROWN, AND COMPANY

In this extremely fascinating book these two authors make an interesting assertion that to me, boggles the mind. "In every industrializing country bitter, often bloody battles broke out between Second Wave industrial and commercial groups and First Wave land owners in alliance, very often, with the church (itself a great landowner) Masses of peasants were forced off the land to provide workers for the new 'Satanic mills' and factories that multiplied over the landscape."(p. 19) "In the United States it required a terrible Civil War for the industrial-commercial interests of the North to vanquish the agrarian elites of the South… Second Wave modernisers triumphed over First Wave traditionalists" (p. 20).

Yet in all the history books the Civil War is portrayed as an enterprise of high moral principles, of compassion, led by the abolitionists whose primary aim was to free the slaves so that they too could enjoy the blessings of freedom. If their (Tefflin) analysis is true, then the Civil War was in reality a monstrous crime engineered by cold-blooded mercenary interests caring only for the almighty dollar. Is this the type of history that Henry Ford referred to as "bunk?"

LINCOLN AND SAVING THE UNION

A letter to Horace Greeley's New York Tribune is cited as revealing Abraham Lincoln's true position on the question of the Union and slavery: "My primary object in this struggle is to save the Union, and it is NOT either to save or destroy slavery. If I could save the Union without freeing ANY slaves. I would do it; and if I could save it by freeing ALL the slaves, I would do it, and if I could save it by freeing some and leaving others slaves, I would also do that."

Here we see Lincoln at his most devious lawyerly best. Although, by implied admission that, slavery versus abolition of slavery was *the* primary reason for the disagreement between the North and the South, he deflects critical analysis by insisting it was instead Union versus Disunion! A question of treason! By doing so he cleverly denies that if the North had not made slavery *the* issue, there would not have been the impulse for the South to their Declaration of Independence or secession. This, as we all know was not the case. It was slavery, (and all its economic ramifications, slave labor was cheaper than free labor) that was *the* driving consideration.

A more accurate, if brutal cold, statement that would truly reflect the reality, goes like this: "My primary object in this struggle is to save the Union, and it is NOT either to spare the Southerners or kill the Southerners. If I could save the Union without killing any Southerners, I would do it. If I could do it by killing all the Southerners, I would do it; and if I could save it by killing some and sparing others, I would also do that."

Thus it all boiled down to clubbing the South into submission to the North's (Lincoln's) authority and if he had to kill *all* the Southerners, he would most certainly do it!

CAUSE

The evidence to support my contention that the issue of slavery was the principle, primary, and perhaps only, cause of the American Civil War is overwhelming and undeniable. As early as October 4, 1854, at the Illinois State Fair Abraham Lincoln delivered a passionate speech against the extension of slavery: "Slavery is founded on the selfishness of man's nature, opposition to it in his love of justice. These principles are in eternal antagonism, and when brought into collision so fiercely as slavery extension brings them, shocks and throes and convulsions must ceaselessly follow. Repeal the Missouri Compromise, repeal all the compromises; repeal the Declaration of Independence; repeal all history—you still cannot repeal human nature It will still be the abundance of man's heart that slavery extension is wrong, and out of the abundance of his heart his mouth will continue to speak."

The turmoil of Missouri, Kansas, and Nebraska all centered and revolved around the issue of slavery. The violence there was a repeated reminder of the passions aroused, and it was all about slavery, slavery, slavery! Then in June 1858, there was Lincoln's magnum opus the House Divided speech… again centered on the troublesome issue of slavery! Then from August to October 1858, we have the seven nationally reported debates with Stephen Douglas from which Lincoln was thrust into the national spotlight because of his antislavery oratory. And then there was the raid on Harper's Ferry by John Brown, an event that galvanized the South and focused their attention on the threat to their farm machinery: the slaves!

The greatest bamboozlement by the Lincoln administration was the clever characterization that slavery was not the cause of the Civil War for this would be resisted by a significant percentage of the North: instead the nation was frightened into supporting Lincoln by the clever, oft-repeated lie that secession and disunion would ultimately prove catastrophic as it would lead to the failure of that noble experiment: democracy. Too late did the draft rioters of New York, July 1863, come to realize they had been had. They soon cowered into obedience once over 1,000 of their friends were butchered by crack Union soldiers fresh from the bloody fields of Gettysburg.

SLAVERY: THE PRIMARY ISSUE

Virtually all the historical presentations on the Civil War are deliberately designed for the reader to focus his/her attention on the lie that the threat of disunion or secession was *the* proximate provocation that required the North to act so forcefully to forestall such an earth-shattering calamity. As they cry "treason" at the secessionists, they move heaven and earth to keep your eyes fixed on this goal to justify their actions against a reluctant, just now created enemy. They would have you believe that the Civil War was not for such an ignoble, paltry consideration as the abolition of slavery!

To deny that slavery was *the* major issue, *the* bone of contention, *the* major source of friction between the North and South is to deny a lot of obvious and apparent history that preceded this calamitous event. Starting with the Ordinance of 1787, or the Northwest Ordinance, which, among other matters, also banned slavery in these areas and revealed the hidden agenda which the North was embarking upon. Then there was the Missouri Compromise of 1820, which allowed Missouri to enter the Union as a slave state only on the condition that Maine, a recently created entity, be simultaneously admitted as a free state. Then there was the Wilmot Proviso which attempted to ban slavery in the recently acquired "new territories" from the war with Mexico. Slavery had been an accepted fact in Texas but not in Mexico. The Compromise of 1850 also centered on the issue of slavery, admitting California as a free state and deferred action on Utah and New Mexico. Again, the hot potato issue of slavery dogged the politicians and they introduced the disastrous "popular sovereignty" concept in the Kansas-Nebraska Act which, in passing, also repealed the Missouri Compromise. Thus, we see by this long list of significant legislation, the centrality of slavery as *the* preeminent contentious issue between the North and South, and it was *this* issue that caused the Civil War (despite all the bullshit you hear from contrary historians).

The noted historian, Bernard De Voto, observed, "At some time between August, December 1846, the Civil War had begun." Also, "David Wilmot, safeguarding the conquests of his party's war President, had made A. Lincoln President of the United States."

CAUSES

The historical community has exhibited remarkable, nay fantastic, abilities at mental gymnastics, at contortionism of unprecedented magnitude, in explaining the cause(s) of the American Civil War. All the while, many examples are found to clearly indicate why the North waged war upon the South, none is clearer than Lincoln's House Divided speech, and since he became the most powerful man in these United States, it is his opinion that matters.

"A house divided against itself cannot stand."
"I believe this Government cannot endure permanently, half slave and half free."
"I do not expect the Union to be dissolved- I don't expect the house to fall—but I do expect it will cease to be divided."
"It will become all one thing or all the other."

The firmness of his resolve is clearly revealed in these short, simple, and direct sentences and none but the most obtuse could fail to see war coming. The rapid response by the South in declaring their secession (Declaration of Independence, Phase II) tells us they did not fail in getting this message. War was coming and they were ready! The dogs of war were let loose and could not be stopped short of the apocalypse that eventually transpired to the everlasting shame of those who precipitated it—the abolitionists, Harriet Beecher Stowe, but mostly Abraham Lincoln!

I would have imagined that the above utterances by Lincoln would dispel any and all equivocations as to the cause of the War for *their theories don't count*. Only the thunderbolts from the White House count in the real world. All others are mere inconsequent abstractions and must be dismissed as such! We are told that actions speak louder than words and his were deafening! The issue was slavery! Slavery! Slavery! All else flowed inexorably from this significant source till it became a raging river of blood, death and destruction.

Supporting his thesis a political cartoon in Harper's Weekly, October 11, 1862, shows a man, representing the South, up a tree labeled "*slavery*" and Lincoln with an axe saying: "Now if you don't come down I'll cut this tree from under you." But, as I have said before, the clincher was when Lincoln met Harriet Beecher Stowe in the White House and said, "So this is the lady who wrote the book that made this great war."

SECESSION CHARACTERIZED AS A DIVORCE

Virtually every survey of the American populace ranks Abraham Lincoln as a noble and heroic figure unfortunately struck down by assassination. He is often regarded as one of our greatest Presidents. The spinmeisters, historians, propagandists, and bullshitters have assiduously followed this portrait which was firmly imprinted into the American lexicon by his political colleagues. Then his assassination, the ultimate tragedy for creating the image of martyr, solidified his place in the pantheon of heroes. My attempt to debunk this image begins in pointing out the plain unvarnished fact that he was an attorney and a politician, hardly the characteristics of a saint! In addition, he possessed another odious feature that of a perennial political wannabe, flitting in and out of politics but always careful to be in the loop, ready at a moment's notice to jump into the political arena. These alone in a normal world should disqualify his candidacy for sainthood. But those were not normal times.

In my opinion Abraham Lincoln was an excellent "scribbler," a polished debater and, by all accounts, a very good lawyer, but his executive abilities in the most powerful seat in the United States—president—were sadly lacking. In a statesman, as opposed to a politician, one might expect a person with a mental outlook capable of compromise, conciliation, accommodation, and a give-and-take attitude essential for political success. Lincoln, however, seemed to have lacked these prerequisites, preferring tactics characteristic with those inured to power politics, where an iron will leadership backed by a larger population and superior industrial might produce an overwhelming military machine that crushes everything in its path. Lincoln, thus, showed the ruthlessness and cunning of a student of Machiavelli! Exhibiting these characteristics, he is, therefore, revealed to the world as a virtual dictator!

Divorce from the North by the South because of irreconcilable difference was anathema to the narrow legalistic mind of Lincoln. This "marriage" was virtually made in heaven and Lincoln insisted "let no man put asunder." The incompatible parties would be forced to remain wedded and live out their lives in continuous friction and misery even if he had to virtually kill every unwilling Southerner to perpetuate this insanity! With a murderous intensity he pushed his generals toward ultimate victory, then proudly proclaim he had "saved the Union" while standing on a pile of 1,000,000 American corpses, a ghastly image and grotesque beyond words!

REASONS FOR THE CIVIL WAR—WAR BETWEEN THE STATES, WAR OF NORTHERN AGGRESSION, WAR BETWEEN BROTHERS, LINCOLN'S MADNESS

SUMMARY

II. PRESERVE THE UNION

"*Preserve the Union*" became the rallying cry and the mantra of the North combined with a sense of urgency to convince the nation that a successful secession would lead to the most horrendous and cataclysmic of catastrophes—the failure of that rare and noble experiment. Democracy, with a subsequent collapse of the republic and with it American civilization! Immediate suppression was, therefore, paramount! How dare these upstarts act in such a way as to cause the nation to smash into unrecognizable smithereens? The Union was a sacred inviolable marriage between two dissimilar, and perhaps incompatible, cultures—the clever, aggressive, acquisitive, industrial, and capitalistic North, and the primarily aristocratic, agrarian, and laid-back South. The combination however, resulted in a larger fighting force that greatly enhanced the likelihood of success of opposing the British. (It should be mentioned here that in the discussions by the Continental Congress the issue of slavery was deliberately avoided, fearing alienation of the Southern delegates.) In time, once the Union was firmly established, and the British were vanquished, the troublesome and nagging issue of slavery could be raised without fear of major repercussions. In essence the South had been snookered!) Had not the North convinced the South of the need for their participation, the enterprise (revolution) would have failed, the leaders hung for treason, the United States would be a part of the British Commonwealth, and we would undoubtedly be speaking English with a distinctly British accent!

Charging the South with "treason" was another clever propaganda ploy by the North to put them on a psychological defensive. The fact that one partner in the "marriage" requested a divorce was an insult to the North.

Subconsciously, perhaps, Lincoln was merely following his father's strongly held tenets, "When you make a bad bargain, cling to it all the more tightly." The North and the South were radically different societies, thrown together out of necessity to fight the British but basically incompatible and, therefore, qualifies as a "bad bargain." Lincoln would hold on to the South, and not let it go even if he had to kill all its inhabitants to preserve it. Once Lincoln embarked on the war he would persist and persist, determined to see the war to its bloody and horrific pyrrhic ending, again "clinging to it all the more tightly."

Freedom, equality, and justice.

II. ABOLITION OF SLAVERY

"For removal of that wretched contradiction of slavery in a nation originally dedicated to the inalienable rights of man." Lincoln

Predicated upon a purely humanitarian concern, the abolitionists, progressively more and more stridently, repeated the accusation that "slavery was a sin in the sight of God," using a technique that was later used with such great effect by that notorious propagandist, Joseph Goebbels. Even a cursory examination of the Bible by a novice or by any dispassionate reader will reveal this assertion to be nothing but an outright lie and clever fabrication. Everywhere that slavery is mentioned in the Bible the references are without exception positive and supportive as slavery was a common and matter-of-fact occurrence and practice in that world. To conclude otherwise requires an effort of enormous mental gymnastics or, as I suspect, outright prevarication. Considering that the majority of the abolitionists were leaders in the Christian community and, therefore, must have had more than casual familiarity with the Bible then it becomes logical to conclude that, for whatever reason, they were lying! Therefore, by progressive logical steps, we determine that all the activity by the abolitionists was of sheerest deception, a deliberate design to cover up the truth by the most malignant, the most villainous, the most horrendous falsehood, that their motives to liberate the slaves were the most honorable, pure, and altruistic.

Without slavery friction between the North and South would not have created such heated and violent exchanges as had occurred prior to the outbreak of the Civil War. There would not have been a Mason-Dixon line, no Missouri Compromise, no Kansas Nebraska Act and all the attendant ramifications, and most assuredly, no John Brown! As the South felt obliged to extend slavery into the New Territories to keep the cotton industry and, therefore, the Southern economy going, the North felt obliged to resist these moves. Back and forth it went with ever-escalating rhetoric and anger culminating in the physical violence upon a house member, Charles Sumner. The election of Abraham Lincoln, his views were well-known in the South, was the last straw. The South knew that with the election of this man they were now in a life-or-death struggle to preserve their economy and, therefore, their way of life.

III. WRECK SOUTH'S ECONOMY

As we read the history books on the Civil War focusing primarily upon its causes, a large amount of skepticism is needed to overcome the clever characterization of that war as noble crusade undertaken by compassionate people to achieve a just conclusion. No matter how intense the propaganda, a careful dispassionate analysis will lead an honest person to conclude that *the* major aim of the Civil War was to wreck the South's economy! The history books incessantly claim precipitation was caused by the efforts of the abolitionists and their fellow travelers to bestow the blessings of liberty and freedom upon the noble African savages who were cruelly exploited by the vicious and mean Southern planter class.

As we study and observe the evolution of the American colonies it becomes apparent that, although they had a major commonality in that they were primarily pioneers of Anglo-Saxon background there arose in their evolution distinctive and very different characteristics. The bipolarity of the country was remarkable in that the North became a "Yankee"-dominated, aggressive, capitalistic, industrial society while the South took on the characteristics partially of the Northern country of aristocratic outlook but primarily agrarian. As the industrial giant of Europe, Britain, relied on the colonies to provide raw materials to their hungry factories for processing and selling back to the colonies, so too did the North rely on the South for a similar arrangement. With the same arrogance as Britain, they virtually demanded the South to deliver them the raw materials, rice, tobacco, and especially cotton, to their water-driven efficient factories.

The American South had supplied three-fourths of the raw cotton for Britain's textile industry, the very heart of the British industrial economy, but by 1862, such cotton imports had fallen to one-half of the 1860 level. Even though this had led to a "cotton famine" and widespread unemployment in Britain, the British prime minister, Viscount Palmerston, and his cabinet failed to act in the best interest of their economy. Had they recognized the Confederacy as a sovereign nation and assisted their liberation from Northern domination, they would have assured the uninterrupted flow of cotton to their mills. Instead of standing by their "brothers" in the South (linked by a strong sense of linguistic, cultural, and historic ties) and instead of ignoring the plight of the mill owners, they caved in to the political demands of the populace whose sympathetic views on slavery trumped employment in the mills and avoidance of starvation.

Had the South been successful in achieving their independence from Northern domination and exploitation those characteristics, that made the original colonies successful, would have been perpetuated and extended by the peoples of the South—knowledge, enterprise, and confidence. It would not have eventuated, as the alarmists in the North successfully convinced the nation, in the collapse of civilization, or the failure of that noble experiment, democracy! Two nations, side by side, would have existed peacefully to compete with and to complement the other's weaknesses, all the while maintaining that interdependence that had existed from day one. Does not the amicable relationship between America and Canada support this viewpoint?

Unfortunately this was not to be. The abolitionists and their fellow travelers carefully and cleverly cultivated the minds of the citizenry by an incessant barrage of propaganda that slavery is a sin in the eyes of God and must be eradicated. Once this was done the flow of cotton would be restored to the hungry cotton mills of the North run by exploited cheap immigrant labor, Slavery was deemed an evil, but was not the liberation of 4 million illiterate, uneducated, unprepared, landless, and penniless Negroes into a hostile environment not a greater evil?

Once the mindset was prepared, the next step was to elect a saintly figure, in the form of Abraham Lincoln (by schemers and plotters in smoke-filled rooms), to operate the great levers of power. The issue would be resolved, not by compromise nor by negotiation but by the worst imaginable carnage America had ever seen, even to this very day. Military power, an extension of Lincoln's purported physical strength, would decimate the South and cow the rest into abject submission. The question in my mind arises: should not this terrible carnage have triggered the dilemma in the minds of any historian of any worth. What price, submission? What price, emancipation? Instead the prevailing view glosses over the terrible reality by insisting the war to be justifiable (homicide). It should boggle the mind of every thinking human being.

JUDGMENT AND SUMMARY

PROCEEDINGS BEFORE THE COURT OF ABSOLUTE MORALITY, HONESTY, AND INTEGRITY

Ladies and gentlemen of the Jury: We, the prosecution, stand before you charging the members of the abolitionist movements with deliberate genocide and crimes against humanity! Possessed by supreme arrogance, illusions of moral superiority, excessive compassion toward the Negro slave, naivety and pious zealotry, they did instigate against the legitimate slave industry, did arouse and incite the passions of the citizens of this peaceful nation to rise up and make bloody war upon the Southern states. Further, they did make false claim that this relationship of master owning and controlling another human as his slave, a known human exploitation of man by man since the dawn of civilization, as suddenly an abomination and a Sin in the eyes of God! Yet when one cares to look at the Bible, no evidence can be found to support this claim! None! But on the other hand we can and do find a definite biblical proscription in that Commandment that says, "Thou shalt not kill," a commandment grossly breeched and conveniently ignored by all those who participated in the Civil War!

Further, we charge specifically Samuel Gridley Howe and his cabal of the Secret Six of Boston who did surreptitiously plan, finance and support the madman and "loser" John Brown in his raid on Harper's Ferry, dramatizing the assault as a blow for freedom on behalf of the downtrodden Negro slaves. Added with this group we include reformers-in-residence Frederick Douglass, William Lloyd Garrison, Julia Ward Howe, and the world's greatest and most successful propagandist in the annals of propaganda: Harriet Beecher Stowe!

But foremost, we charge Abraham Lincoln, a successful backwoods lawyer with a checkered political career who achieved the pinnacle of the presidency by clever behind-the-scenes manipulators who connived in smoke-filled rooms. As a remarkable scribbler and debater he prepared the nation for the inevitable confrontation with the South, but totally lacking in the political skills of diplomacy, where tact and compromise are paramount requisites for success, he blundered into the most catastrophic carnage to ever face the nation. As a result of this stupidity the nation wasted over 600,000 lives, the flower of American youth for the paltry success of abolition of slavery. What price, emancipation?

Lastly we charge these same miscreants with the second greatest coup of the nineteenth century, (after instigating the Civil War) and that is the cover-up of this dastardly deed. To this very day the received wisdom is that slavery was a sin, greater than that of Adam and Eve in Eden, greater than that of Cain killing Abel, and that sin could be only rectified and cleansed by the Civil War, a noble crusade on behalf of humanity (or put more plainly, justifiable homicide) But they were lying sons of bitches and no one called them to account because they were too stupid to recognize that they had been bamboozled!

SUMMARY, PEACEFUL SEPARATION VERSUS FORCED UNION

1. Dual and dissimilar economies with the South agrarian and staple-producing, and the North a land of traders and manufacturers.
2. Dual and dissimilar societies with the South maintaining the British aristocratic outlook and the North a hard-nosed business Yankee trader outlook.
3. No real union of common interests between them.
4. The Continent was most certainly large enough for two mighty empires.
5. The result of a peaceful separation would result in distinct but friendly communities on both sides of the separating border, rather than forced intercourse between unwilling partners and the North would serve as the New Canaan or refuge replacing Canada as a safe haven.
6. The inconclusive issue of State's rights on the one hand suggesting separation as an understood right of a disgruntled and unhappy participant. The North denied it even though the Constitution seemed to allow it.
7. An independent South does less harm to the North and as much good as before. If they were separated there was less chance of "contamination" from slavery, i.e., effectively quarantined
8. Honor was no longer compatible with submission as it would mean subjugation.

FORCED UNION BY THE NORTH

1. "The Union must be preserved" was an emotional appeal based on a sense of historical consciousness or pioneer feeling of togetherness.
2. The historical trust must be maintained!
3. The interpretation by the North was that the Constitution did not

allow secession and, therefore, the South must be compelled to abide by the signed agreement.
4. Fear of European pressures upon a divided people.
5. The religious argument: God has placed us here to make one great nation and it was our responsibility to fulfill his purpose.
6. The foundations of history must not be tampered with or destroyed by selfish people more interested in their own personal comfort and prosperity.
7. Fear of an epidemic of secessions resulting in a cluster of defenseless principalities.
8. Exploitation of one man by another, as in slavery was a sin (and moral imperative). This view of the North must be communicated to the South and convince them of their transgressions.

DECLARATION

To summarize, Jefferson set out three major, but basic, ideas in the Declaration of Independence: (1) God made all men equal and gave them the right to life, liberty, and the pursuit of happiness. (2) The major task of government is to protect these rights. And (3) if a government attempts to deny these rights, the people can revolt and establish a new government.

On June 7, 1776, Virginia's Richard Henry Lee introduced a congressional resolution that declared, "These United Colonies are, and of a right ought to be, free and independent states, that they are absolved from any allegiance to the British Crown, and that all political connection between them and Great Britain ought to be totally dissolved."

INDEX

A

abolitionism, 107
abolitionists, x, xxiii, 4, 49, 101, 104–5, 116–17, 120, 124, 126–27, 203
Abolitionist Union Humane Society, 122
Adams, John, 133
Alarming History of Medicine, The (Gordon), 27
Alexander the Great, 161, 194
Amazing Grace (movie), 127–28
American Civil War, vi–viii, x, xiv, xvii–xviii, 4–5, 29, 32, 35, 124, 126, 232, 234, 236
    as an Armageddon, 10
    causes of, 43, 241–42, 244–46, 251, 257, 267
    cost of, 3, 6–7
    start of, 189
    true character of, xx, 4, 15
American Holocaust, 125, 159, 232
American Revolution, 39, 42, 49, 70, 72, 81, 165
Anderson, Perry, xiii
Anderson, Robert, 189
antislavery movement, 119
Argentina, 42
Aristotle, xvi, 101, 181

B

Bagehot, Walter, 157
"Battle Hymn of the Republic" (Howe), 119, 198
Beard, Charles, x
Bell, John, 131
Biden, Joseph, 85
Bierce, Ambrose, 235
Bork, Robert, 85
Bradford, William, 44

Brady, Mathew, 13
Brazil, 42
Breckenridge, John C., 131
"British Rights of Man, The" (Locke), 41
Brown, John, 119, 143, 152, 251, 259, 265
Browning, Orville Hickman, 189
Buchanan, George, 36
Burke, Edmund, 62
    "Reflections on the Revolution in France," 62
Butler, Benjamin, 227
Butler, Samuel, xx, 35

C

Cameron, Simon, 137
Carter, Boake, xiii
Carwardine, Richard, 173
Cato, 108
Catton, Bruce, xiv
Chase, Salmon, 158
Chicago Convention, 16
Christianity, 121
civilization, 35
civil liberty, 55
"Common Sense" (Paine), 60
Connolly, Cyril, 35
constitution, 64
Convention of Virginia, 47
Cooper, James Fenimore, 50
    "On American Equality," 50
Cromwell, Oliver, 155
Curtis, Benjamin R., 155
Czechoslovakia, vii–viii

D

Dana, Charles A., 31, 222
Davis, David, 137, 139

Davis, Jefferson, 85, 92
DeBow, James B. D., 91
Declaration of the Rights of Man and Citizen, 39
democracy, 81
dictator, 152
Disuniting of America, The (Schlesinger), 21, 23
Divine Right of Kings, 39
Dom Pedro II, 128
Douglas, Frederick, xv
Douglas, Stephen A., 75, 131, 149
Dublin, 112

E

Emancipation Proclamation, 145
Emerson, Ralph Waldo, 119
English Common Law, 44
"An Exhortation and Caution to Friends Concerning Buying or Keeping of Negroes" (Keith), 118

F

fanatic, 107
Ford, Gerald, 87
Ford, Henry, viii, xxiii, 249
Fox, Gustavus, 189
freedom, 47
French Revolution, 39, 72, 81
Fugitive Slave Law, 14

G

Garrison, William Lloyd, 127, 247, 265
"Genius of Universal Emancipation, The" (Lundy), 122
George III (king), 49, 103, 191
Germantown Protest, 118
Gettysburg Address (Lincoln), 78, 151, 245
Gladstone, William, 191
Glorious Revolution, 39
Goebbels, Joseph, xxiv, 160, 203, 205, 209, 211, 258

Gomes, Peter, 35
Goodwin, Doris Kearns, 139
Gordon, Richard, 27
  Alarming History of Medicine, The, 27
Grant, Ulysses Simpson, 12, 217, 222
Great Awakening, 118
Greeley, Horace, 31, 222, 250

H

Halstead, Murat, 137
Hamilton, Alexander, 16
Hanks, John, 135, 140
Hanna, Marcus Alonzo, 136
Hart, B. H. Liddell, 228
Hart, Michael H., 247
  100, The: A Ranking of the Most Influential Persons In History, 247
Hartfield, John, 236
Havel, Vaclav, viii
Helsinki Final Act, 87
Henry, Patrick, 94
Herndon, William Henry, 134
higher law, 48, 109, 116, 119, 126
historians, 21, 205
history, viii, x, xxiii, 21–22, 24, 26, 35
Hitchens, Christopher, vi, xiii, 163
Hitler, Adolf, xxiv, 7, 31, 137, 178
Hoffer, Eric, 24
Holmes, Oliver Wendell, Jr., 232
Holy Grail, 34
Hook, Sydney, 235
"House Divided" (Lincoln), 149
House of Burgesses, 44
Howe, Julia Ward, 119, 198, 265
  "Battle Hymn of the Republic," 119, 198
Howe, Samuel Gridley, 265
human nature, 28

I

imaginative horror, 242

Imperial Presidency, The (Schlesinger), 155
Individuals and Their Rights (Machan), 66
In Flanders fields the poppies blow (McCrae), xii
inner light, 122, 124

J

Jamestown, 44, 47, 108
Jefferson, Thomas, 48–50, 54, 61, 66, 78, 133
Judd, Norman B., 137
Julius Caesar, xxv

K

Kansas-Nebraska Act, 75, 252
Keith, George, 118
    "An Exhortation and Caution to Friends Concerning Buying or Keeping of Negroes," 118
Keynes, John Maynard, 176
king, 36
kingmakers, 136–37, 139
Kosovo, 11

L

Lamon, William Hill, 137
Lane Theological Seminary, 210
Lee, Richard Henry, 269
Lee, Robert E., 96
Legree, Simon, xxiv
Liberty has sometimes, 87
Lincoln, Abraham, viii, xiii, xvi, 3, 5, 15, 83, 86, 103, 105, 128, 157–59
    of skills as an attorney, 181
    "bad bargain" philosophy of, 151
    calls for abolition of slavery, 103
    character of, 174–77, 179, 255
    as a debater, 187
    declaration of war of, 231
    dictatorship of, 153–55, 157, 159–60, 162–63, 171, 195
    1860 election of, 9
    failures of, 82, 85, 87, 131
    first inaugural address, 242
    as front man of the abolitionist movement, 143
    Gettysburg Address, 78, 151, 245
    "Holy Grail" of, 34
    House Divided, 149
    hypocrisy of, 184
    involvement in the Civil War, 220
    legacy of, 172
    literature on, 179
    Machiavellian behavior of, xxi, xxiv
    obsession of, 51, 186
    orders execution of Sioux Indians, 30
    presidential nomination of, 139–41
    propaganda about, 203, 207
    as a secular saint, 32
Lincoln, Mary Todd, 227
Lincolnmania, ix, xxiii
Lincoln Memorial, 172
Locke, John, 57, 59, 61, 66, 69, 77–78, 81, 84, 242
    "British Rights of Man, The," 41
    "Two Treatises of Government," 54
Logan, John A., 184
lost generation, 15
Lundy, Benjamin, 122
    "Genius of Universal Emancipation, The," 122

M

Machan, Tibor, 66
    Individuals and Their Rights, 66
Machiavelli, Niccolo, xxi
Magna Carta, 36, 39
Martin Van Buren, 16
Marx, Karl, 66
Mayflower, 44
Mayflower Compact, 44

McCoy, Rosanna, 236
McCrae, John, xii
    In Flanders fields the poppies blow, xii
McGlellan, George, 217
McKinley, William, 136
Medill, Joseph, 134
Methodism, 127
Mexico, 42
Mill, John Stuart, 26
    "On Liberty," 26
Missouri Compromise, 75, 251–52, 259

N

nation-states, 68, 77
natural liberty, 55
natural rights, 41, 48, 55, 57, 61–63, 66, 73, 79, 84–86, 184, 220
Nicholson, Virginia, 15

O

"On American Equality" (Cooper), 50
100, The: A Ranking of the Most Influential Persons In History (Hart), 247
"On Liberty" (Mill), 26
Os, Amos, 107

P

Paine, Thomas, 59–60, 62
    "Common Sense," 60
    Rights of Man, The, 62
Parker, Theodore, 28, 119
Parkhurst, Sylvia, 35
Petition of Right, 39
Pilgrims, 44
Plato, 21, 66, 101
Pol Pot, 7, 31, 154, 159
Prochaska, Frank, 157
Pyrrhus, 237

Q

Quakers, 122, 124

R

Randall, James G., x, 193
Ray, Charles, 134
Reagan, Ronald, 47
Reeves, Richard, 35
"Reflections on the Revolution in France" (Burke), 62
republicanism, 75, 94
rhetoric, xxiv, 16, 83, 106, 181, 203, 259
rights, 41, 57, 62, 67, 72, 75, 79, 85
Rights of Man, The (Paine), 62
Roosevelt, Quentin, 35
Roosevelt, Teddy, 35
Rousseau, Jean Jacques, 41, 55, 81
Russell, John, 191

S

Salmond, Alex, 80
Sandburg, Carl, xviii, 237
Scepter, 63
Schaub, Diana, 71
Schlesinger, Arthur M., Jr., x, 22–23, 234
    Disuniting of America, The, 21, 23
    Imperial Presidency, The, 155
Scott, Winfield, 189, 247
secession, 54
Second Great Awakening, 118
self-government, 66
Sen, Amartya, 82
Seward, William, 48, 158
Sharansky, Natan, 46
Shaw, George Bernard, 10, 35, 179, 235
Sheridan, Philip Henry, 219
Sherman, William Tecumseh, 218
Shiloh (Pittsburgh Landing), 12
Sigel, Franz, 227
sin, 110
slavery, xiii, xxiii, 4, 9, 251–52
    abolition of, 5, 7–8, 23, 103, 105, 127–28, 166, 237, 252, 258
    in the Bible, 109, 111, 113

as cause of American Civil War, 252–53
history of, 106, 108, 165–66
and religion, 115–16
social contract, 55, 69, 73, 81
social contract theory, 36
society, 55
Solitude of Self (Stanton), 73
Stalin, Joseph, 7, 31, 117, 178
Stanton, Edwin M., viii, xiii, 123, 155, 158–59, 205, 222
Stanton, Elizabeth Cady, 73
Solitude of Self, 73
states, 36
Stowe, Edward, 211
Stowe, Harriet Beecher, xix, xxiv, 111, 124, 185, 209–12, 254
Uncle Tom's Cabin, 210
Strong, George Templeton, 16
Sumter, Fort, 4, 153, 189
surplus women, 15
Sydenham, Thomas, 27

T

Tempest, David, 28
terrorism, 228
"Thoughts on Slavery" (Wesley), 127
Toffler, Alvin, 248
War and Antiwar, 248
Toffler, Heidi, 248
War and Antiwar, 248

Toleration Acts, 39
Treaty of Union, 80
Twain, Mark, 87
"Two Treatises of Government" (Locke), 54

U

Underground Railroad, 115
United States of America, xvi, 14, 81, 106, 133, 242

V

Vidal, Gore, 244–45
Virginia Company, 44
Voto, Bernard de, 235, 252

W

War and Antiwar (Toffler), 248
Washington, George, 133, 231
Weed, Thurlow, 141
Welles, Gideon, 92
Wesley, John, 127, 211
"Thoughts on Slavery," 127
Wilberforce, William, 127–28, 157
Will, George, 77, 180
Williams, Roger, 125
William the Conqueror, 63
Wilmot, David, 252
Wilson, Woodrow, vii, 94
Woolman, John, 119

Edwards Brothers Malloy
Thorofare, NJ USA
May 31, 2012